THE POWER OF
LETTING GO

THE POWER OF LETTING GO

HOW TO DROP EVERYTHING THAT'S HOLDING YOU BACK

JOHN PURKISS

aster

An Hachette UK Company
www.hachette.co.uk

First published in Great Britain in 2020 by Aster,
an imprint of Octopus Publishing Group Ltd
Carmelite House, 50 Victoria Embankment
London EC4Y 0DZ
www.octopusbooks.co.uk

Text copyright © John Purkiss 2020
Design and layout copyright © Octopus Publishing Group Ltd 2020

Distributed in the US by Hachette Book Group
1290 Avenue of the Americas, 4th and 5th Floors
New York, NY 10104

Distributed in Canada by Canadian Manda Group
664 Annette St., Toronto, Ontario, Canada M6S 2C8

ISBN 978-1-78325-363-0
A CIP catalogue record for this book is available from the British Library.
Printed and bound in the UK

19

Consultant Publisher: Kate Adams
Art Director: Yasia Williams
Editor: Ella Parsons
Copy Editor: Charlotte Cole
Assistant Production Manager: Lucy Carter

CONTENTS

FOR THE MAGICIAN IN ALL OF US

INTRODUCTION

DISCOVER A NEW WAY TO LIVE

What do you want to change in your life? Maybe you want better health, a relationship, happier relationships, a better job or more money. Or maybe you want less of something, like stress, frustration or problems with your boss. Maybe you've been trying to change your life for years, but it still hasn't happened – which has left you feeling stuck.

This book will show you how to live life on another level. You'll see yourself and the world around you in a completely different way. You'll let go of years of conditioning, which have led you to believe that the only way to make things happen is to think hard, take lots of action and keep going through thick and thin. If you follow the steps described in this book, things will happen much more easily, with a lot less stress.

You don't need to control everything that's happening. You don't need to push, struggle, fight, force things or try to manipulate people in order to make things the way you want them to be. It's exhausting and unnecessary.

If you let go in the way I'm going to describe in this book, you'll experience what's often called flow. You'll find yourself working in sync with the world instead of fighting against it. When you let go your intuition will become much stronger. While it's OK to have a plan, it's also essential to tune in to what's actually happening and work *with* it instead of *against* it. You'll be much more successful at whatever you choose to do.

I studied economics at Cambridge and worked in banking and management consultancy. Then I did my MBA at INSEAD in France and co-founded a software company. These days I recruit senior executives and board members. In my work I've often been surrounded by engineers, scientists, accountants and lawyers, most of whom have been trained to think a lot and analyse things. If we're not careful, we start to see ourselves as body/mind machines. The mind has thoughts which the body then attempts to translate into action and results. A friend of mine once said – only half-joking – that his body's role was to transport his brain from one meeting to the next.

Just because we've been trained to think doesn't mean we're thinking machines. Artificial intelligence will automate many processes currently performed by humans. There's an urgent need for us to discover who we really are – and a new way of living and working.

Fortunately, the Vedic tradition in India figured out the solution thousands of years ago. The Vedas are the origin of mindfulness, yoga, Ayurvedic food and medicine, Transcendental Meditation® and much more. (*Veda* is a Sanskrit word meaning knowledge. Mindfulness, which has become very popular in the West, is often associated with Buddhism. Both Buddhism and Hinduism have their roots in the Vedic culture, which predates the Buddha.) These Vedic techniques have filtered through into Western culture and millions of us have benefited from them. However, the underlying philosophy and effectiveness of the knowledge have been lost for most people.

The problem with the way that mindfulness and yoga are often practised in the West is that they help us to work harder and harder without burning out, at least in the short term. I know people who meditate in the toilets at work. We've acquired the techniques without the philosophy. Then we wonder why life is so stressful and frustrating.

So what's the underlying philosophy? Here's my take on it, as it applies to living the life you really want:

- Your brain and body are part of something extremely intelligent. We can see this intelligence in every aspect of nature, including plants, animals, humans, planets and stars. The whole thing is amazing, and it keeps evolving. For simplicity, let's call it Existence.

- We make the mistake of thinking we're separate from Existence. We believe we're a particular body and mind – separate from everyone and everything else. This identification with the body/mind is known as ego. (It isn't the ego described in Freudian psychology, as I'll explain later.) Instead of flowing with Existence, we fight it or try to control it. Instead of enjoying life, we keep getting stressed and frustrated. In our efforts to get what we want – and avoid what we don't – we create conflict with other people and damage our environment.

- Once we let go of the ego – that is the belief that we're separate from everyone and everything else – life is much easier. It's the ego that keeps fighting for survival, creating dramas and making life stressful. Once you let go of it, you'll discover that you're more than you ever imagined yourself to be. Life will unfold naturally, with little or no stress. I'll guide you through the process step by step. The more you let go, the better things will go.

What do you want to change?

Let's go back to what you want to change in your life. Most of us have three categories of desire:

1. Things you wanted to happen which have happened. (We often overlook these.)

2. Things you *didn't* want to happen which have happened.
3. Things you want to happen which haven't happened yet (often despite a huge amount of effort).

Maybe 2 and 3 ring a bell for you. Many of us are worried or feel stuck in one or more areas of our lives. The four key areas are:

1. Health
2. Relationships
3. Career
4. Money.

We tend to keep getting stuck in our own particular way. Here are some examples:

- A wealthy person who's professionally successful but keeps falling sick.
- Someone who's professionally successful and has been divorced several times.
- Someone who's good at what they do but doesn't have enough work or money.
- A calm, healthy person who enjoys loving relationships and is always broke.
- A calm, healthy person who earns plenty of money but can't find the right partner.

These patterns of 'stuckness' aren't random. If you relocated to some place thousands of miles away you'd probably find yourself feeling stuck in the same way as before.

The reason each of us is stuck in some areas but not others is that we all have particular *pain patterns*. I'll give you exercises to help you identify and let go of yours.

At some point we let go completely. In other words, we *surrender*. When you surrender you let go of the ego. So who are you? You're *pure awareness*, *pure consciousness*, *pure presence* or *pure being*. In Vedic terminology you're the *Self* with a capital S.

How does all this relate to the things you *want* to happen which *haven't happened yet*? The point is that many of us try to *force* things to happen. You may have lots of positive thoughts about what you *want* to happen. You may also take lots of action to try and *make* it happen. And everything stays more or less the same.

Once you let go completely – or surrender – there's no ego left to do the forcing. Desires are then realized easily from pure being/pure consciousness/pure awareness/pure presence. This is the great paradox of letting go.

Here's the process:

1. **A desire arises**
2. **You surrender and experience oneness with your true self, which is consciousness**
3. **The resistance within you falls away and you're free to take action**
4. **The desire is fulfilled easily and spontaneously.**

LETTING GO
Once you surrender, your intuition will tell you what to do

You'll have a feeling about people you meet and situations in which you find yourself. You'll have a strong sense of what to do next. There'll be lots of helpful coincidences.

- **You take the right action at the right time, efficiently and without stress.**
- **You still think and analyse when you need to, but thinking is your servant, not your master.**
- **You allow things to work out in ways you could never have imagined.**

Letting go doesn't mean giving up

A common misperception is that letting go is the same as giving up. The reality is that once your intuition kicks in, you may find yourself taking a lot *more* action than before. It will also be much more effective and aligned with your true purpose. Your ego will no longer get in the way of what needs to be done. Taking action will be fulfilling instead of stressful.

You may also be concerned that you won't care about other people. In fact, the opposite happens. The more we let go of the mental junk we've been carrying around in our heads, the easier it is to be present and give people our full attention – and tune into their feelings.

You can let go in three stages

Some people let go in one big jump. One day they're ordinary human beings. The next day they're enlightened and doing things which are widely regarded as miracles. But for most of us, letting go is a more gradual process.

We gradually drop everything that's holding us back. Right now you may not even be *aware* of what's holding you back. It may be something small and subtle, but it can still prevent you from enjoying life and fulfilling your potential.

In this book I'm going to keep things simple by describing three stages:

1. **Let go of thoughts,** including judgements, labels, expectations and stories. For example, you realize that your mind keeps creating problems by chattering on about something that has no relevance to what's happening now. You learn to witness – or observe – the thoughts and let them go. Now you can get on with life.

2. **Let go of pain,** which is provoked by a constant stream of negative thoughts. For example, there may be a painful memory which makes it very hard for you to live life to the full. You re-live the experience and allow yourself to *feel* the pain, suffering, discomfort or agitation. It gradually dies down, and is highly likely to disappear. Your mind is clearer and you feel much better.

3. **Surrender and tune in to something far more intelligent than your brain.** Now that you've let go of the past and the future, you fall into the present. You follow your intuition and naturally take the right action at the right time. Everything happens more easily.

Good things happen when you let go

Whatever your starting point may be, letting go makes life much better. The more you let go, the more you'll find that:

- You feel relaxed and forget to worry.
- You understand intuitively what's going on around you.
- Creativity becomes a natural part of life.
- Things fall into place.
- You take the right action at the right time.
- There's little or no stress.

- Your health improves.
- Relationships are easy.
- Earning money is no longer the main aim, but it happens more easily.
- You're no longer bored. Life is exciting again.
- You allow other people to be as they are.
- You laugh more.

Once you let go, your desires can be met easily and without stress. I'll show you how.

Letting go is good for your health

As you may have noticed when I listed the four areas of our lives, health was top of the list – before relationships, career and money. There are two reasons for this:

1. Once you let go, you're likely to start feeling better quickly.
2. When our health improves, it usually leads to improvements in other areas of our lives.

Among the techniques I'm going to discuss in this book are mindfulness and Transcendental Meditation, whose benefits have been well documented in scientific studies.

Letting go is for everyone

This book draws on spiritual traditions which go back thousands of years. I've spent over 20 years exploring them, so you don't have to. I've attended retreats and learned several types of meditation. (I've also experienced other phenomena such as kundalini awakening and yogic powers, otherwise known as *shaktis.*) Everything I've tried that works involves letting go.

In the meantime I've taught other people, who've enjoyed similar results. You can learn and start applying the material in this book right away. Please note that you won't need to change your religion, or any views you may hold *about* religion. Letting go is for everyone.

Make your own discoveries

Science is widely misunderstood. Some people 'believe in science' the way others 'believe in religion'. But science isn't a belief system, it's a method of enquiry. The *scientific method* is ultimately about letting go of all the flawed theories and explanations that our minds make up in a systematic fashion. We can never *prove* something to be true. We can only discover what's false, thereby getting closer to the truth.

My recommendation is that you simply try the exercises in this book and see what happens. Just give it a go.

Some of the exercises require a few minutes of dedicated time. You can practise the others in the middle of whatever else you're doing. They've worked for large numbers of people, but not every exercise works for everyone. Try each one for yourself as you read this book. In some cases you may notice a difference – or learn something – right away. In other cases, nothing may happen, at least initially, so I suggest you move on and come back to it later. An exercise that does nothing for you the first time you try it may prove very useful later on.

If you do the exercises thoroughly, you'll start noticing benefits in every area of your life.

You've already started letting go

Most of us have at least *some* experience of letting go. Here are some examples:

- You wake up gently without an alarm. You feel completely relaxed after a long sleep. For a few seconds you're barely conscious and there aren't any thoughts. You don't even know who you are or where you are. Gradually you become aware of your body lying in the bed. You may have some thoughts about what time it is, what day it is or what you're supposed to be doing today. Maybe you think about making some tea or coffee and having breakfast. Pretty soon you're moving around, having lots of thoughts and taking action.

- You're standing on top of a mountain, gazing at the beautiful scenery. You let go. Your mind falls silent for a few seconds while you take it all in. It feels blissful. Then the thoughts start up again: 'This is a bit like that other mountain last summer...', 'Should I take a photograph?', 'Who are those people over there?', 'Is it time for lunch?'

- You're sitting there meditating, with your attention on your breath. Your mind keeps wandering, so you keep bringing your attention back to the breath. Eventually you get fed up with it and stop trying to meditate. Suddenly the thoughts stop, if only for a few seconds. You're conscious, but there aren't any thoughts. Then you think to yourself, 'I've stopped thinking.' There you go – the thoughts have started up again. But let's not overlook what happened. For a few seconds, you let go.

- You're in the midst of yoga when suddenly you forget about yourself. There's only the breath. You let go and flow from one *asana* (pose) to another.

- You've learned Transcendental Meditation. You hear the *mantra* in your mind and you let go. At some point there's only consciousness. You *are*, without any thoughts. It may last for a few seconds or several minutes. There's no effort – only bliss.

- You've been trying really hard to make something work. It could be a job, a business, a relationship or some creative project. You're mentally and emotionally drained by all the effort you've been putting in, trying to make things happen. Eventually you let go. You allow things to be as they are. You take a break from endless thinking and doing. What a relief!

- You're completely absorbed in some activity that you really enjoy. It could be dancing, making a model aircraft or playing with a child. Whatever it is, you forget about yourself and lose track of time.

- You're playing a sport such as football, tennis or rugby. You've been practising hard for weeks. Now you let go and enjoy the game. Your mind goes quiet. Time seems to slow down. For a few seconds or more, one action flows into another, with no mental commentary.

- You've come to the end of a one-hour yoga session. You're lying on your back, exhausted, in *shavasana* (corpse pose). You let go completely. For a few blissful seconds, your mind is empty.

If you've experienced anything like the situations I've described above, then you've already started letting go. It's just that most of us only let go for a few seconds or minutes each day. The rest of the time, we do the opposite. We wrestle with the thoughts that appear in our minds while our emotions yo-yo up and down. We try to control what's happening. Life is frustrating and stressful when it really doesn't need to be.

The good news is that you can let go all the time

You don't have to be on top of a mountain, in a yoga pose or deep in meditation to let go. You can let go all day long, right where you are, doing whatever you're doing. That's what this book is all about. It may sound scary at first, but it's the most natural thing in the world. I'll show you how to do it, step by step. Once you settle into it, you'll wonder why you ever tried living any other way. When we let go completely we're more fulfilled than ever before – with little or no stress.

Let's get started.

SUMMARY

- You may be trying hard to make changes in your life, but feel stuck. If you follow the steps in this book, things will happen much more easily.

- You'll find yourself working in sync with the world instead of fighting against it – your intuition will become much stronger.

- The Vedic tradition tells us that every aspect of nature, including our brain and body, is part of something extremely intelligent, which I'll call Existence.

- Instead of flowing with Existence, many of us fight it, creating conflict with other people and our environment.

- Once we let go of the ego that fights for survival, life will unfold naturally, with little or no stress.

- We're often stuck in one of four key areas of our lives: health, relationships, career or money.

- This book will show you how to let go in three steps. You'll learn to let go of thoughts, let go of pain patterns and then to surrender and tune in to something far more intelligent than your brain.

- When we surrender and let go of the ego, we fall into the present. Then your intuition tells you what to do and desires are realized much more easily.

- You'll still think and analyse when you need to, but thinking will be your servant, not your master.

- Letting go is good for your health.

- Letting go is for everyone, whatever their religion may be – if they have one.

- Most of us have already experienced letting go. This book will help you let go all the time.

1

BE PRESENT AND ENJOY
EACH MOMENT

Being present is essential preparation for the three key steps in this book, which are to:

1. **Let go of thoughts**
2. **Let go of pain**
3. **Let go completely.**

You're physically present all the time – it's only your attention that wanders. Buddhists call this the *monkey mind*. Left to its own devices, our attention runs around, out of control. Being present simply means that we bring our attention back to the present moment. It sounds simple, but putting it into practice requires a specific technique.

HOW TO MEDITATE SUCCESSFULLY

I meet lots of people who tell me they tried meditation and gave up. Some say they tried without any instructions (which makes me wonder how they learned to drive), but most of them just say they found it impossible to control their minds. These days, more and more people are learning meditation using apps on their mobile phones.

Just so you know what you're up against, try this:

'Trying to meditate'

Sit in a quiet place where you won't be disturbed. Switch off your phone. Close your eyes. For the next five minutes, stop thinking.

How did you get on? You may well have found it impossible to stop thinking for more than a few seconds. After a while, a thought appears, then another, then another. Pretty soon you're thinking about the future or the past, or about what may be happening somewhere else right now.

A lot of people think meditation is about emptying the mind, but most of us find that impossible – at least initially. So what's the answer?

The secret of meditation is to give the mind something to do

An easy way to get started

Sit in a quiet place where you won't be disturbed. Switch off your phone and take off your watch. Close your eyes.

Now turn your attention inwards. Place your attention on your breath as it flows in and out.

Every time your attention wanders, bring it gently back to the breath. There's no need to judge yourself – it's all part of the process. Just relax and bring your attention back to the breath.

Carry on doing this for several minutes.

Now open your eyes. What do you notice? How do you feel? Do you notice any difference in the sounds, colours or shapes around you?

Some people say that colours appear brighter. Many people feel much calmer. Sounds or shapes may become clearer to you. You may also notice other sensations throughout your body.

This exercise gives your mind something to do, which is to keep paying attention to the breath as it flows in and out. Every time your attention wanders, you bring it back to your breath.

If you keep doing this on a regular basis you'll find it becomes easier to be present – to remain in the here and now.

It's pointless to judge yourself when your attention wanders. The wandering and coming back are all part of the process. Every time your attention wanders, just bring it gently back to the breath.

In the introduction I asked you what you wanted to change in your life. (You may have found yourself thinking about that during the exercise just now.) The more you let go, the more easily the change will happen. I'll show you how to do it. For the time being, all you need to do is notice the thoughts and then bring your attention gently back to the breath.

We can now extend this exercise from your breath to your five senses.

Connect with your senses

Find a quiet place where you won't be disturbed.

Sit upright on a chair, completely relaxed. Place your hands on your thighs and your feet flat on the floor. Close your eyes.

Allow your body to relax. Let go of any tension. Let go of any concerns or preoccupations.

Place your attention on the breath as it flows in and out. Every time your attention wanders, bring it gently back to your breath.

Now feel the air on your face. Be aware of this for a while.

Now feel the weight of your body on the chair. Be aware of this for a while.

Every time your attention wanders, bring it gently back.

Now feel the touch of your feet on the ground. Be aware of this for a while.

Listen as far as possible into the distance, beyond the sounds nearby. Be aware of this for a while.

Let go of any mental comments or judgements about the sounds.

Now bring your attention back to the breath as it flows in and out.

Every time your attention wanders, bring it gently back to your breath.

This is based on an exercise which I learned at the School of Philosophy and Economic Science, and which – according to tradition – goes back thousands of years.

While you were doing the last two exercises, you may have noticed now and then that there weren't any thoughts. You were conscious, but there weren't any thoughts. Maybe it only lasted for a second or two. As soon as you realize 'I've stopped thinking', that's another thought. That gap between thoughts was pure consciousness.

Spiritual teachers often use the analogy of a screen in a cinema. The screen is consciousness, and it's there all the time. Thoughts and feelings are like images which are projected onto the screen.

We get so caught up in the thoughts and feelings that we forget about the screen. If someone switches off the projector, we notice the screen again.

I'll say a lot more about pure consciousness later in this book. If you haven't experienced the gap between thoughts yet, it isn't a problem. Each of us has different experiences at different times, but we're all on the same journey.

It's fine to glance at your watch occasionally while you're meditating. Then you can bring your attention back to the breath. When people meditate in groups, there's often someone who keeps track of time, ringing a bell at the beginning and the end.

Stand back and observe the thoughts as they come and go

Many of us believe we *are* our thoughts – and behave accordingly. We have a happy thought, so we feel happy. We have a sad thought, so we feel sad. In other words, we *identify* with our thoughts. It's like being a puppet on a string. Allowing ourselves to be controlled by our thoughts gets us into all kinds of trouble, ranging from lost career opportunities to broken relationships to road rage.

Maybe you're feeling stressed about what someone has said, or a problem you can't solve. Maybe you're on a crowded train, feeling uncomfortable and frustrated, while other people's behaviour is annoying you. In all these situations we naturally experience a stream of thoughts and emotions.

The question is: what are you going to do about it? Are you going to get annoyed? What else can you do?

The solution is to stand back from your thoughts and observe them as they come and go. Being present will help you.

- If you can observe something, it isn't you.
- You're the *observer*, not the thought or feeling (such as discomfort, frustration or annoyance).

Pause

Close your eyes if it's safe to do so. Otherwise, place your attention on an object in front of you.

Now feel the breath moving slowly in and out of your body. Feel the weight of your body on the chair, and then the touch of your feet on the floor. Now feel the texture of whatever your hands are touching.

Every time your attention wanders, bring it gently back to one of your senses. If you feel angry or frustrated, notice that feeling and then bring your attention back to your senses.

I'm not asking you to deny or repress any thoughts or feelings that may come up. All we're doing is noticing them, and then bringing our attention back to our senses. Now try this:

- Notice each thought as it appears.

- Don't try to do anything about it. Don't judge it, resist it or push it away.

- Just witness it, observe it.

- In a while the thought will disappear, and another thought will come. Just let them come and go.

THE IMPORTANCE OF BEING PRESENT

Being present will help you avoid making decisions which you later regret

The psychologist Carl Jung once said, 'when an inner situation is not made conscious, it happens outside, as fate.' The more present you are, the easier it'll be to observe thoughts and then decide whether you're going to act on them.

You'll become more and more aware of what's going on around you – and in your mind. You're much less likely to be a victim of 'fate'.

Being present reduces stress

Stress is resisting what is. We observe what's happening and judge it as wrong. Then we get frustrated, angry or depressed about it. The more upset we become, the harder it is to do anything to change the situation.

In chapter 3, I'll show you how to let go of the pain which is *causing* the stressful thoughts. In the meantime, all you need to do is keep returning to the present moment – by placing your attention on your breath, for example. The stressful thoughts will naturally begin to die down.

As you observe any stressful thoughts, place your attention on the breath. Allow further thoughts to come and go.

Then you can take the right action at the right time.

Being present helps us let go of fear

Many of us are afraid of heights, particularly when we're climbing a ladder or walking across a tall bridge. It's perfectly natural. One way to deal with it is to place your attention on your breath and on the sensations beneath your hands and feet. This will move your attention away from fearful thoughts. At the same time, you'll stay focused on what really matters: where you're placing your hands and feet.

Being present helps us stay safe

In the three years before I learned to be present, I had three minor car accidents. I was so focused on my goals that I missed what was happening in that particular moment. Once I'd learned to be present I tuned in and naturally anticipated what was likely to happen, on the road and elsewhere.

Being present helps us stay cool

When we learn to be present and observe our thoughts as they come and go, it's much easier to deal with difficult people. We no longer react to their moods and behaviour in the same old ways.

A few months after learning to be present, I was working for a director of a company. She was very talented and successful, but also volatile. Every now and then she would fly into a rage, with no warning. The people around her were often stressed.

One day her secretary phoned me and said the director was very angry and wanted to see me. If this had happened a year earlier, my mind would have been flooded with thoughts about why she might be angry and what was going to happen to me. I would have thought about all this on the way to her office, imagining how the conversation would turn out and getting more and more wound up about it.

Instead, I remembered what I'd learned about being present. I placed my attention on my breath and felt it moving slowly in and out of my body. Every time my attention wandered, I brought it gently back to the breath. While I was walking down the corridor, I noticed the temperature and pressure of the air around me, and observed my surroundings in detail: the thick carpet, the wooden panelling, the ornate ceiling.

When I arrived at the director's office, my attention was in the present. I'd let go of any chaotic thoughts and emotions. I just listened to her with an open mind, which had given up trying to anticipate what would happen. She was furious, but she probably sensed that her anger was having little or no effect on me. Once she'd finished speaking I replied calmly, without fear or anticipation. I gave her the facts she needed. The conversation flowed relatively smoothly and easily. We agreed on the action to be taken, then I went back to my office and got on with it.

Practise being present

Think of a situation in which you find someone's mood or behaviour stressful.

Now you have a choice: you can either allow your mind to run wild, or you can be present.

If you keep your attention on your breath, your senses and your surroundings, you'll remain in the present moment. You won't become nearly as stressed.

I noticed that the less I reacted to other people's moods, the more my relationships improved.

It can feel strange at first when you stop reacting to other people's moods. It may even feel insensitive or selfish, but you can still love people and have compassion for them. Their anger and frustration make them suffer, both mentally and physically.

When we change, people around us also change

While I was working hard and getting nowhere, my mum was naturally stressed about it. After I learned to let go and be present, she also became calmer and our relationship quickly improved. A couple of months later, I was offered a well-paid job, which removed a major cause of the stress.

You don't have to join in the drama

One day I was travelling with some bulky and heavy equipment for a conference, and I was late when I hauled my bags onto the airport bus. A man was standing inside the bus next to the luggage rack. I asked him to move down, but he refused, so I picked up all my bags and placed them on top of the suitcases that were already on the rack.

'What the f**k is wrong with you?' he shouted. 'Nothing,' I said. I stood there calmly, placing my attention on my breath.

I could feel my pulse accelerating, but I kept returning my attention to my breath, and to the weight of my feet on the floor of the bus, which by now was winding its way up to the airport. By the time we arrived at the terminal, the man had calmed down and my pulse had returned to normal. We all disembarked and headed towards the check-in counters.

Stand back – watch the thoughts and emotions come and go

Sometimes thoughts and emotions come thick and fast, particularly if someone has criticized you or tried to harm you. When this happens, it's best to stand back from it all. Try this:

- Imagine that it's raining hard and you're standing on a bridge over a river which is close to bursting its banks. The swirling water is your mind in chaos. The river is becoming more and more dangerous, carrying all kinds of debris with it. There are branches from dead trees, wooden planks and car tyres caught in the swell.

- The debris is your thoughts and emotions. There may be unpleasant memories of what someone said about you, maybe a few negative thoughts you've had about yourself and about what might go wrong now. Along with the thoughts comes a stream of negative emotions such as anger, sadness, regret and the feeling you're not good enough. They all come sweeping down the river.

- There's no need for you to reach down and grab hold of them. If you do so, you may be dragged along and swept away. All you have to do is be present. Feel the weight of your feet on the bridge. Feel the sensations in your body and the breath flowing in and out. If you're standing when you do this exercise, stand with your feet slightly apart. Imagine the thoughts and emotions rushing by beneath you. Imagine you're resting your hands on the wall of the bridge, and looking down into the water. Feel the stone wall beneath your hands.

> • Whenever you get distracted, bring your attention back to your breath. Breathe slowly and deeply. Place your attention within your body. Observe the thoughts and emotions – allow them to come and go.

With a bit of practice you'll notice a big change. Instead of being upset, you'll *observe your mind* being upset. Instead of being confused, you'll *observe your mind* being confused. And so on.

Being present will improve your relationships

When we're listening to what someone is saying, we tend to have thoughts about what *we're* going to say in response. We may also think about what we'd do in their situation and how we can help them. Maybe we start evaluating what they're saying and begin to formulate a counter-argument. The point is, we aren't really listening. At the very most, we're *listening in order to respond.*

It's better to keep returning to the present when you're with someone. The first step is to make sure you're present before a meeting, an interview, a party or a meal with a friend. If you're present at the beginning, it makes it easier to keep returning to the present.

Being present will make you better at sport

Some sportspeople experience *the zone*, in which everything seems to slow down. They instinctively make the right move at the right time, without needing to think about it.

Here's an example from a friend who's a keen golfer:

I remember that day ten years ago as if it was yesterday. A friend and I had decided to spend the day playing golf. The plan was to play nine holes in the morning, break for lunch, and play another eighteen in the afternoon.

The morning game was an ordinary round. However, it allowed me to develop a good feel for the course, and to visualize the fairways and greens clearly. Trusting the knowledge of the course I'd acquired in the morning, I set out to play in the afternoon with a carefree mindset.

I remember being in a very quiet place. There was no internal dialogue, and no criticism or judgement.

The focus was on letting go of the score and just being in the moment. Everything seemed to happen naturally and instinctively, a bit like being on cruise control. It was the lowest score I'd ever shot.

Being present will make you a better presenter

If you're going to speak to a large audience, try the following exercise.

Be present before a presentation

Make sure you're present before going on stage or on camera. You'll literally have more presence and you'll connect with your audience.

Feel the weight of your feet on the floor and place your attention on your breath now and then. This will help to ensure that you aren't carried away by your own material.

Whenever I'm going to speak at a live event, I like to turn up half an hour to an hour beforehand and chat to members of the audience who've also arrived early. They tell me about their work, their hobbies and the things they're most interested in. In many cases we discover something in common, whether it's a place we've visited or a problem we've been dealing with. I learn their first names and write them down before I start my presentation. All of this requires me to be present and listen carefully.

When I start the presentation, I already know several people in the audience and some of them are keen to join in. I use a minimum of PowerPoint and spend as much time as possible on exercises. Being present and engaging with people makes everything go well.

I invite you to try this for yourself.

Being present will make your intuition stronger

The *Encarta World English Dictionary* defines intuition as 'immediate insight without reasoning'. Many people believe – or assume – that intuition is purely a matter of experience. Herbert A Simon, who won the Nobel Prize for economics, said that 'Intuition is nothing more and nothing less than recognition.' This assertion is reflected in the work of Daniel Kahneman (another Nobel laureate and author of the bestseller *Thinking Fast and Slow*) and Malcolm Gladwell, who wrote *Blink: The Power of Thinking without Thinking*.

It's clear that recognition can have *something* to do with it. For instance, first-class footballers and tennis players have lots of practice and experience of watching a ball travel through the air and hit the ground. With this experience, they are able to recognize which way a ball is likely to bounce without having to think about it (there's no time for thinking anyway).

Similarly, now that I've worked in executive search for many years, I'm able to recognize patterns in people's behaviour, which really helps me in my job. But I disagree with the assertion that intuition is nothing more or less than recognition. Once I'd learned to be present, my intuition switched on like a searchlight. I suddenly began to understand people much better. I knew exactly which candidate was likely to fit with each client, in terms of personal chemistry and working style.

But that doesn't necessarily mean that intuition *always* involves pattern recognition. Even in the case of footballers and tennis players, there may be something else going on – such as when sportspeople 'get into the zone', as I described earlier.

Two years before this book was published, I suddenly began to experience much more of what you might call the *intuitive spectrum*. Here's an example. I've visited HDH Sri Nithyananda Paramashivam – known to his followers as Swamiji (see pages 187 and 197) – several times on his ashram and elsewhere in India. I've seen people do some extraordinary things in India and the UK, but let's stick to what I've experienced personally. Please note that I have no medical training beyond a first-aid badge in the Scouts.

While I was working on this book Swamiji initiated me and others into a *shakti* (yogic power) known as *body scanning*. This isn't the Buddhist practice of scanning your body as a form of meditation. We were asked to scan *other people's* bodies from head to toe – over a period of two minutes – and say where they had some sort of problem.

I scanned the first ten people on four separate occasions. It was 90 per cent accurate in nine cases with complete strangers. In one case I scanned someone I knew and it was less than 50 per cent accurate. (I had lots of thoughts about what might be wrong, based on information I'd assembled from meeting him three times before.)

In one case I scanned an Indian man and said, 'There's a problem with your heart, your urinary tract and your feet.' ('Urinary tract' isn't a phrase I'd normally use. I didn't know where it was until I googled it afterwards.) He said he'd had an operation on a hole in his heart a few years earlier, and had a urinary tract infection right now. There was also a medical problem with his feet which I didn't understand.

Please note that I didn't 'see' the physical conditions. I just *knew* they were there. Maybe you can understand now why I don't believe that intuition is purely a function of experience and pattern recognition. This might seem incredible, but I can give you many other examples.

Whether we realize it or not, we are all somewhere on the intuitive spectrum, and this isn't a fixed ability. If you do the exercises in this book, your intuition will become stronger and stronger.

MINDFULNESS AND MEDITATION

The exercises I've shown you so far in the book could be described as *mindfulness*. You keep returning your attention to the present – every time it wanders, you bring it gently back.

If you practise mindfulness a couple of times a day – sitting on your own in a quiet place – it will gradually spill over into your whole life.

Each activity is an opportunity to keep your attention in the here and now. You could be washing the dishes or walking down the street.

Practise mindfulness during the day

Stand up and walk around slowly. Feel your feet pressing into the ground and the breath flowing in and out of your body.

Every now and then you may notice that your attention has wandered. Suddenly you're immersed in thoughts about the past or the future, or what might be happening somewhere else right now.

As soon as you notice this, bring your attention back to the present using one of your senses. One way is to press your thumbnails into your forefingers. A bit of discomfort can be useful – it gets our attention.

Transcendental Meditation

Transcendental Meditation was introduced to the West in 1959 by Maharishi Mahesh Yogi. It is a simple, natural, effortless technique that you practise twice a day for twenty minutes. The word *transcendence* may sound a bit wacky at first, but millions of people have experienced this state through TM. When we *transcend*, we *go beyond* the ordinary state of waking consciousness. Suddenly there are no thoughts. There's only consciousness.

TM is a completely different kind of meditation technique to mindfulness. As with mindfulness, TM involves giving the mind something to do. In this case we use a *mantra*, which is a tool for meditation. (*Mantra* is a Sanskrit term meaning *mind instrument*.)

When you learn TM you receive a personal mantra from your teacher along with the technique for using it in a natural and effortless way.

When I attended an introductory talk, our teacher Neil Lukover explained that TM allows the mind to settle down so the body settles down, giving us deep rest. As a result, 'the body is deeply rested, and the mind is lively'. He called it *restful alertness*. The programme I'd joined consisted of four sessions. In between, we practised on our own.

Everyone's experience is different. The first few times I found it difficult, but then things suddenly began to happen. It felt like gentle electric pulses crossing my scalp from one side to the other. Then I naturally began to *let go* during the meditation (they call it *going deep*). It felt like falling feet first into a deep pool while continuing to breathe normally. As Neil had predicted, there were times when the mantra dropped away, leaving me in the state of *no thought, no mantra*. It was bliss.

Once I'd mastered the simple technique, it was effortless. I also noticed that if I didn't meditate for a day or so, I felt a bit stale. Then if I meditated, I felt refreshed. It was like a river that silted up and then began to flow again.

I've since found that TM removes around 90 per cent of the jet lag I used to experience. Sometime after learning it I flew from London to Shanghai. It used to take up to four days for my body to adjust completely after a long-haul flight. As usual, I ate the meals they put in front of me and slept as much as I could, but the big difference came when I was awake and unable to sleep. Whenever I was tired of reading I would stop and practise TM for 20 minutes.

I arrived at my hotel in Shanghai relatively well rested, and then slept for a couple of hours. After that I was fine, with almost no jet lag. The same thing happened on my trip back to London.

TM gives us the experience of oneness

Essentially, *oneness* means there's no separation. After I learned TM I felt a stronger connection with people and animals. Some animals are closely connected with members of their own species. Shoals of fish and flocks of birds can travel in dense formations and then turn in an instant, without bumping into each other. Human beings are usually much less coordinated, but occasionally something remarkable happens. (I must warn you not to try this yourself.)

One day I was on a Tube train in London, on my way to a meeting with the founder of a software company. I was standing in one of the carriages, reading the news. Other people were standing or sitting: some were chatting, others were silent.

A man in his 60s was sitting on one of the benches opposite another man who looked around 20. Every now and then, the older man criticized the younger one under his breath – and the younger one swore back at him, becoming angrier each time.

I had a feeling that the younger man was about to beat up the older one in front of many other passengers, but no one moved or said anything.

Then, within a few seconds, several of us were lying on top of the younger man, who was flat on his face on the bench. I was closest to his left ear and said, 'Don't do anything. You'll go to jail.'

A few seconds later, we all climbed off him again – and went back to reading and so on. No one said anything.

At the next stop he stood up, muttered something, then stepped off the train and onto the platform. After he left, no one made any comment.

I've since described this episode to a friend who was in the army. He said I was mad, we could've been stabbed. But we acted simultaneously, without any planning or communication. It all happened in an instant.

Ideas and solutions come from *not* thinking

Maybe you've experienced something like this:

- You work on a problem until you get stuck and can't go any further.
- You do something physical such as walking, swimming or playing sport.
- The solution comes to you in a flash, either during the activity or shortly afterwards when you look at the problem again.

When has a solution appeared after you stopped thinking and let go? Write it down to remind yourself.

There's strong scientific evidence for the benefits of meditation

There are many meditation teachers with scientific backgrounds, including those mentioned in this book:

Name	Degree subject
Ajahn Brahm	Theoretical physics
Jon Kabat-Zinn	Molecular biology
Maharishi Mahesh Yogi	Physics
Shamash Alidina	Chemical engineering

Thousands of research papers have been published on the subject of meditation and mindfulness. Here are two examples:

- In a Massachusetts General Hospital study, published in the *Journal of Clinical Psychiatry*, 93 individuals with Generalized Anxiety Disorder (GAD) were randomly assigned to either (a) mindfulness-based stress reduction (MBSR) or (b) stress-management education (SME). The MSBR group was associated with a significantly greater reduction in anxiety.

- Dr Robert Schneider and colleagues found, in a study published in the *American Journal of Cardiology*, that older people with high blood pressure who practised Transcendental Meditation had a 23 per cent reduction in all-cause mortality and a 30 per cent reduction in cardiovascular deaths compared to control subjects.

YOU *ARE*

Practices such as mindfulness, Transcendental Meditation and yoga all help us to think a lot less in our daily lives and just *be*. We begin to return to our original state.

As babies we simply *are* – we radiate love. As we grow up, we start to *identify* with all kinds of things. We start to believe that we *are* our bodies, which can make us obsessed with each change that occurs and afraid of death. Many of us believe that we *are* the mind – the endless mental chatter that demands a response, with the compulsion to analyse everyone and everything.

We identify with all kinds of other things: our education, social background, ethnicity, nationality, religious beliefs, relationships, occupation, income, wealth and physical possessions.

Think about it for a moment. You were none of these things when you were born. You'll let go of all of them when you die. So what happens in between? Who are you if you aren't that pile of stuff you keep identifying with?

The answer is that you're *pure consciousness*, which you may experience for a few seconds if you wake up gently without an alarm. Then – within a few seconds – your mind will start chattering about your concerns, responsibilities, tea, coffee, breakfast and so on.

Consciousness is there in the background all the time. As I mentioned previously, it's like the screen in a cinema. The film flickers on the screen for an hour or two and we feel as though we're in the film. We get caught up in the drama, which can be fun – or highly distressing. We forget that we're the screen, silent and unchanging.

If you meditate correctly, you may experience pure consciousness. There's no identity – no John Purkiss or Frida Smith – no thoughts or beliefs, no story about what's happened, is happening or will happen. There's just consciousness.

'I am'

While you're walking around, or sitting somewhere, keep thinking one thought: 'I am'.

If any other thoughts occur to you – which they almost certainly will – go back to this thought.

If you notice that you've started to identify, let go. Return to the thought, 'I am'.

Keep thinking it over and over again, like a mantra. (It *is* a mantra.)

That's it. Simple, but surprisingly powerful if you persist. People have used this exercise to reach enlightenment.

Please note that you aren't saying 'I am this' or 'I am that'. You're saying, 'I am'. In other words, you aren't identifying with anything. You simply are.

This is a radical change. You are. Everything else comes and goes.

Use the 'I am' mantra

You can use this mantra anywhere, at any time. Here are two examples:

- If you're engaged in some vigorous activity such as running, try thinking 'I am' over and over again. You may notice the 'I am' coinciding with the in- and out-breaths, while your body carries on doing what it needs to do.

- If your mind goes into overdrive, speculating about what might happen or could happen, focus simply on 'I am'. If you keep your mind focused on 'I am', you may find that the torrent of thoughts dies down.

All the techniques described in this chapter will help you to be present. This allows life to unfold naturally, including the things you want to happen.

SUMMARY

- Left to its own devices, our attention runs around, out of control. Being present means bringing our attention back to the present moment.

- It's very hard to stop thinking. It's better to give your mind something to do.

- Sit and relax, and bring your attention to your breath. When your attention wanders, just bring it back to your breath. This exercise is described fully on page 30.

- You can then bring your attention to the five senses. This exercise is described on page 33.

- When there's a gap between thoughts, that's pure consciousness. It's like a cinema screen, there all the time while projected images – thoughts and feelings – come and go.

- Don't judge your thoughts and feelings. Just observe them. You'll notice that they disappear, then new thoughts and feelings come.

- Being present in this way can help you see things clearly before you decide to act. It reduces stress. It also helps us let go of fear, stay safe, keep cool and enjoy harmonious relationships. It will make you better at sport and at presenting to an audience.

- Mindfulness, yoga and Transcendental Meditation can all help us to be present and let go.

- 'I am' is a useful mantra for being present and letting go of your identity.

2

LET GO OF THE
THOUGHTS THAT
KEEP YOU STUCK

Once you've learned to be present and observe your thoughts, you can start letting go of them.

You may be wondering why this is a good idea. The answer is that repetitive thoughts keep you stuck and prevent things from happening in your life. Here are some examples:

- **Thoughts about the past**
- **Thoughts about the future, including worries and *if only*s**
- **Stories**
- **Labels**
- **Judgements**
- **Expectations**
- **Comparisons**
- **Opinions**
- **Conclusions**
- **Conspiracy theories.**

These thoughts prevent us from seeing and hearing what's going on, absorbing information and exploring new opportunities. They block our intuition and stop useful ideas from coming to us. When we let go of repetitive thoughts, we allow things to happen in new and exciting ways.

LET GO OF THOUGHTS ABOUT THE PAST

Our thoughts and feelings about the past get in the way of what's happening now. Letting go of them creates space for new things to happen.

Small children are fascinated when they see something for the first time. It could be a dog, a cat, a flower, a tree, a puddle, a thunderstorm or a sunset. By the time we reach adulthood, we've collected a long list of experiences relating to everything around us, from dogs to sunsets.

When we see a sunset now, or a dog comes up to us, we automatically have thoughts about the past. We *associate* what's happening with some previous experience. When you see a sunset you may start thinking about a holiday a few years ago and who you were with at the time. If a dog comes up to you, you may think about your own dog who died when you were 12 and how sad you were about it.

Constantly connecting the present with the past prevents us from experiencing life as it unfolds. It can also feel dull and heavy. It's usually easier to observe this in other people than in ourselves. You've probably met someone who keeps reacting to events in the present by talking about the past. You may also have noticed the same tendency in yourself – the past gets in the way of the present. (It's particularly hard to get to know a potential partner if you keep comparing them with your ex.)

Of course, experience is valuable: it helps to inform our decisions. From childhood onwards we learn that dogs bite, nettles sting and so on. If we do something frequently, we start to recognize useful patterns. Having played tennis for a while we learn how the ball bounces, and what the effect of a certain stroke will be. Experience provides us with generalizations about what's *likely* to happen next. You can always draw on your experience if it's relevant, but it's better to make decisions based on what's happening *now*.

Letting go of the past is easier said than done. Our memories are triggered by people, places and the situations in which we find ourselves.

Let go of the past

Next time you're listening to someone, you may notice that your mind has drawn a comparison with the past.

Now you have a choice:

- You could choose to talk about the past. Maybe you can predict which way the conversation will go if you do that.

- You could say nothing about the past. In fact, you could say nothing at all, and then see what happens next. Give it a try.

What happens now?

This exercise takes practice. Someone may say something and then you find yourself talking at length about the past. When this happens, you can simply ask a question and get them talking again. Then listen and see what happens.

If there's a pause in the conversation, *let it be*. Something will happen. It needn't be you talking about the past again.

Space is where new things happen

When we stop making comparisons with the past we create space for something new to happen. This may feel scary at first. Some of us identify strongly with the past: where we were born, our education, work and achievements. The problem is that when we identify with the past, we keep on thinking about it, which makes it very hard to change anything. Everything keeps happening the way it always has, even when we think we really want to change, our past just keeps predicting our future.

I'm not asking you to forget what you've learned, or the experiences you've had. I'm just saying it's best to let go of them and experience what's happening *now* with an open mind.

LET GO OF WORRY ABOUT THE FUTURE

The future isn't a problem. It's only your ego that worries about the future. If you identify with your body/mind then you'll automatically have anxious thoughts about what will happen, what could happen and so on. We've been conditioned to see life as a fight for survival.

This book will help you let go of the ego and experience yourself as consciousness. Then you'll have few, if any, worries about the future. You'll take the right action at the right time, and everything will happen much more easily. In the meantime, the following exercise will help you to start letting go of worry about the future.

Let go of the future

Be clear about what you want to happen. For example, it could be moving to a new house or finding a new job or business opportunity. If you want, you can write it down on paper or assemble some related images to look at.

Please be aware that whatever you keep thinking about will start manifesting in your life sooner or later. (I'll be exploring this from the next chapter onwards.) For this reason, it's very important that you let go of any thoughts about what you *don't* want to happen. If you notice yourself thinking about what you *don't* want to happen, shift your attention quickly to what you *do* want. If you notice yourself talking about what you *don't* want to happen, stop immediately!

Now bring your attention back to the present moment, as I showed you in chapter 1. Let go of all your concerns while you focus on your breath and your senses. Do this every time you feel anxious. You can't be present and worry about the future at the same time, so keep being present.

Your mind may tell you that this is escapism, that you really should be worrying about the future. Ignore your mind, be present and take action instead. The more you remain present, the more clearly your intuition will tell you what to do.

START LETTING GO OF YOUR STORIES

The best way to live is to experience each moment and then let it go. However, most of us don't do that. We label our experiences and assemble them to create stories – about ourselves, other people and the world around us.

We tell these stories to ourselves and to others – and we live by them. Some of our stories are based on painful events in the past, but they shape the present and our future, causing lots more pain.

Some of the stories we tell about ourselves have their uses –

most of us have a story about what we *do*. If someone asks you what you do, it helps if you can give them a snappy answer before they get distracted. If I don't know the person I'm talking to, I usually say something simple like 'I'm a headhunter and I write books'. Or I may say something more specific like 'I'm recruiting a chief executive and completing a book'. Then we talk about whatever interests them.

Most of us need a basic story so we can interact with people and function in society. It's like wearing clothes. Walking around naked doesn't work so well, but it also doesn't help if we become obsessed by our clothes or our stories. There's no need to keep talking about them or allow them to take over our lives. Things become a lot more complicated once we start assembling stories about our *thoughts* and *feelings*. We do this over many years, with the help of our parents, teachers, friends, colleagues and the media. Some stories are positive, but let's start with the negative ones:

- I keep having problems with...
- I may seem to have everything but I'm still unhappy
- I don't want to show off
- People like me don't do that sort of thing
- I used to be successful, but not anymore
- I'm unlucky in love
- I'm a victim of...
- Nothing seems to work
- I'm an outsider
- I'm too old/young
- I'm not good enough
- I feel like a loser
- I can't...

Some people are so immersed that they believe they *are* their stories. They're trapped like characters in a play. Their lives are limited by their stories.

Now it's your turn. What are the negative stories you tell about yourself? Write them down now. If your mind goes blank, you can refer to the list on the previous page for inspiration.

These are your stories, so you can let go of them

You may have several stories, on various topics. It's best to work on them one at a time.

You've probably noticed that I keep referring to these stories as *yours*. That's because, wherever they came from, *you're* the one who chooses to hold on to them – or let them go. This book will help you do the latter. Simply becoming aware that you *have* a story is very helpful.

One day my friend Jacq was driving me to the station when I asked her a question. Here's the essence of our conversation:

Me: What's happening with you?

Jacq: All good except for business. I work hard and I'm always busy, but somehow I'm not making the sort of money I want. It's like there's a glass ceiling on it.

Me: That sounds like a story to me. What are the beliefs behind it?

Jacq: I'm not sure what you mean.

Me: What's the story you tell yourself about you and success?

Jacq: Mmm…Well, when I look at the world what pains me most is the inequality I see. Everything from access to food, money, health, joy and even sporting ability. And if I'm too successful then I guess I'll become one of the perpetrators, one of the baddies creating inequality. (She starts laughing.)

Me: And what do you get out of continuing to tell yourself that story?

Jacq: If I can't get what I want either, then I can continue to think of myself as one of the 'good guys', rather than one of the baddies. Oh dear. I had no idea I was playing to this story…

Me: What would happen if you let go of the belief that you can't get what you want?

Jacq: That would spoil my whole story. (Laughing at herself.) This is hilarious, I'm clear about my values around justice and equality but I had no idea I was holding on to this story. I'm so glad I've got this one out in the open. It's ridiculous.

Me: What would be the benefit of letting go of this story now?

Jacq: Well, I'd probably find life easier to navigate and be more financially successful. Then I'd be able to contribute more money to frontline charities that provide medical care. And if I'm less busy holding myself back, then perhaps I'll have more time and energy to help address other injustices. It's a no-brainer really. I could have been stuck for the rest of my life.

Some of our stories melt away as soon as we look at them closely. Embarrassment and laugher are both helpful.

Eighteen months later, Jacq's life had changed:

> It's amazing. Life is easier in every way, including relationships at home and at work. My business has more than doubled in size. I'm able to give more work to other people and give more money to my favourite charities. Now that life is easier, I'm helping in the Scouting community and looking for ways of doing more elsewhere. There don't seem to be any limits to what I can do now.

If you let go of your stories, you'll allow new things to happen

Let go of your stories

Find a blank sheet of paper, select one of the negative stories you tell about yourself (see page 61), and write down the answers to the following questions:

- What's the story you tell about yourself?

- What are the beliefs underlying your story?

- What short-term pleasure or comfort do you get from holding on to each belief?

- What's the pay-off from telling this story?

- What's this story costing you?

- What will be the benefit to you from letting go of this story now?

As I mentioned, you may have several stories – in which case I recommend you do this exercise for one story at a time. Identify and let go of as many stories as you can.

You may also discover that you have stories about other people

Here are some examples:

- **People are so rude.**
- **Everyone's out for themselves.**
- **They're all a bunch of show-offs.**
- **All politicians are liars.**

Understand your stories about other people

Write down your stories about other people and repeat the exercise:

- What's the story you tell about others?

- What are the beliefs underlying this story?

- What short-term pleasure do you get from holding on to each belief?

- What's the pay-off from telling this story?

- What's this story costing you?

- What will be the benefit to you from letting go of this story now?

Positive stories can be just as limiting

Earlier, I gave you a list of some of the negative stories we might tell about ourselves. Positive stories can be equally limiting, such as 'I'm a winner,' 'I'm an achiever', 'I'm a good father,' or 'I'm intelligent'.

This may be hard to grasp at first, particularly if you grew up in a Western culture – as I did. We've been heavily conditioned to see ourselves as separate, individual body/minds, trying to get what we want in competition with lots of other body/minds.

The reality is that we aren't the body or the mind, since we can observe our bodies and the ever-changing thoughts which we call the mind. We're the observer standing on the bridge. We're consciousness, which never changes. Everything else comes and goes. What I'm doing in this book is showing you how to let go of your identity – as Frida Smith, Fred Jones, or whoever – and live from consciousness, which is infinitely powerful. Any other label which you apply to yourself – even a positive one like 'good father' or 'really intelligent' – is limiting and doesn't reflect who you really are.

For example, if you or I say we're a 'nice person', we're limiting ourselves to a person – a bundle of thoughts and molecules which exists for a few decades, if we're lucky – and will then disappear again like a wave on the ocean.

If you've experienced pure consciousness during meditation or any of the other practices which I'm describing in this book, you'll know that there are times when you're conscious but there aren't any thoughts. All the labels we apply to ourselves drop away. Consciousness is infinite.

If you live from consciousness – and drop your identity as a 'nice person' – you'll experience tremendous fulfilment (and will be on your way to enlightenment). Instead of worrying about your nice-person persona, having to defend it and so on, you can live life to the full. Love, creativity, energy, inspiration and so on will pour out of you. You'll do things you never imagined possible. It's hard for me to describe it to someone who hasn't experienced it yet. All I can suggest is that you take the leap and experience it for yourself. This book is designed to help you do so.

Interrupt your stories by being present

Every time you notice that your mind is telling one of its stories, bring your attention back to the present. Choose an object and focus your attention on it. It could be a building, a tree, a cup or one of your fingernails. Look at it really carefully – study it.

You may notice that the story has stopped. If your mind wanders, the story may start up again. All you have to do is focus your attention on another object and study it. You may notice that the story has stopped again.

I hope you can see by now that your stories aren't real – they're mental chatter. It's a bit like a small child who keeps talking away, trying to get your attention. You can love the child, but you don't have to believe its stories.

Please don't start *analysing* your stories – that will only make them harder to shift. Instead, I'll show you several techniques throughout this book which will help you let them go.

LET GO OF LABELS

Many of us have a habit of labelling ourselves and other people. We say, 'She's a finance person' or 'I'm not an entrepreneur'. In my work I sometimes meet people who've taken a Myers-Briggs test and tell me they're 'an ENTJ'. The test provides 16 boxes and they've jumped into one of them.

As you read this book, you'll start to realize that you're far more than you've ever imagined yourself to be. Labels are very limiting, which is easier to understand when people apply labels to *you*:

Skip the labels

Think back to the last time someone labelled you. How did you feel about it?

Letting go of labels allows people and situations to change and develop. Things happen more easily when we skip the labels.

Let go of the habit of labelling yourself

Earlier in this chapter I gave examples of negative and positive stories we tell about ourselves. Some of them were labels such as *winner*, *loser*, *achiever* and *victim*. There are many other possibilities. Make a list of the labels you've applied to yourself. There may be lots of them.

Now put your pen down and look at what you've written. For each label, ask yourself the following questions:

- Can I be 100 per cent certain that this is true?

- Is there some pay-off from labelling myself in this way? If so, what is it?

- What's the cost of labelling myself?

- When have I lost out by doing so?

Now imagine that you've let go of this label. How do you feel?

Let go of the habit of labelling others

Make a list of the people you've labelled in some way, one below another, down the left-hand side of the page. You can include both individuals and groups of people who share a particular nationality, race or social background.

Now write down the labels you've attached to each of them.

Stop and look at what you've written. Ask yourself the following questions:

- Can I be 100 per cent certain that these labels are accurate?

- Is there some pay-off from labelling people in this way?

- How would these people feel if they found out that I'd labelled them?

- What's the cost to me of labelling these people?

- When have I lost out by doing so?

When we let go of labels, we see people and situations in new and different ways. Relationships improve and we create new ones. New ideas and opportunities come to us.

Avoid labelling those who disagree with you as 'irrational'

When you have a clearly thought-out opinion on something, it's tempting to label anyone who disagrees with you as irrational. The implication is that they're driven purely by emotion or prejudice. This is a common mistake. If you fall into this trap you'll find yourself misinterpreting situations, jumping to conclusions and getting stuck on repeat instead of moving forwards.

When they first encountered suicide bombers in the Middle East, some members of the US military labelled them as irrational. The suicide bombers clearly had different *values*, since they were much more willing to kill civilians. They also had different *assumptions* from the Americans about the requirements for being admitted to heaven. However, based on their values and assumptions, the suicide bombers *were* being rational. They thought they were taking a shortcut to paradise.

If we avoid labelling people and make more effort to understand their values and assumptions, it's much easier to understand what's really happening. Then we can do something about it.

There are many reasons why people could disagree with you and still be rational:

- **Their values might be different from yours.**
- **You and they could have made different assumptions.**
- **They might have had a different experience to you.**
- **They might have information that you don't have – or that you've chosen to ignore.**

Instead of labelling people, it's better to keep an open mind and be curious. I'll talk about that later.

LET GO OF JUDGEMENTS

Many of us have a habit of judging. We label people, events and experiences as 'good' or 'bad', but these mental labels don't exist physically. As Shakespeare wrote in *Hamlet*, 'there is nothing either good or bad, but thinking makes it so.'

If you judge, you suffer

Most of us have had the experience of being frustrated, angry or depressed when we felt that 'things shouldn't be this way' or 'I don't deserve this'.

Here's a simple example. You believe it should be sunny this time of year but it rains, so you say the weather is bad. All we can say objectively is that it's raining. Judging the weather as bad won't achieve anything except to make *you* feel bad. (Living in a country such as the UK provides endless opportunities to learn this lesson.)

Judging the weather may only cause minor suffering, but the same principle applies to other judgements. We can spend years judging family members, colleagues, politicians, national and ethnic groups, and so on. *If you judge you suffer*. It's very hard to do anything constructive when you're frustrated, angry or depressed.

Judgements are futile

Most of us have had an experience which we judged as negative – and were then delighted with the final outcome. Distressing situations can lead to wonderful results. Life unfolds moment by moment, while we make futile judgements about it.

In executive search I can think of several candidates who didn't get a job they really wanted, and went on to be enormously successful elsewhere. They're grateful for the failure which allowed something bigger to happen.

There's a Chinese allegory known as 'The Old Man from the Border Loses a Horse', which has often been repeated and adapted in the West. During the Han Dynasty, an old man named Sai Weng lived near the border, and one day he lost his horse. His neighbours sympathized and said this was very bad luck, but Sai Weng said, 'Maybe losing my horse is not so bad after all.'

The next day the horse returned, with a beautiful mare. The neighbours said this was good luck, but Sai Weng said, 'Maybe this is not such good luck after all.'

His grown-up son loved the mare and rode her every day. One day she was startled by a wild animal and threw him from her back. He broke his leg and couldn't walk. The neighbours said, 'What bad luck!', but the old man said, 'Maybe this is not such a bad thing after all.'

Then war broke out and the emperor's army passed through the border region, recruiting all the young men who were able to fight. Sai Weng's son was no use to them, so they left him in the village to work on the farm with his father.

Sai Weng said, 'Being thrown from the horse saved my son from almost certain death in the war, so it all worked out in the end.'

In China, when something looks like bad news, people often say 'Sai Weng Shi Ma', which means 'The old man loses a horse'.

Allow judgements to come and go – you don't need to talk about them

If you're present you can observe judgements appearing and disappearing in your mind. You don't need to tell anyone about them. You don't need to resist them either – just watch them come and go. Once they go, something new will happen.

Let go of judgements

Notice what's going on around you: the way people speak and behave, the weather, the pace at which things happen, the thoughts which appear in your mind.

If you keep returning to the present, as I described on pages 34–43, you'll start noticing judgements as they appear: 'She shouldn't have said that', 'People shouldn't do that', 'What a stupid situation' and so on.

Instead of clinging to these judgements, just watch them come and go. Make sure you don't resist them – that only makes it harder to let go of them.

After a while the judgements will vanish. New ones may appear – you can let go of them too.

LET GO OF THE NEED TO BE RIGHT

Here's a revealing exercise which I enjoy using in workshops. You can try it yourself with some friends or colleagues. First of all, I pick some controversial questions, such as:

- Should ordinary citizens be allowed to carry guns?
- Should immigration be stopped?
- Should everyone be vegetarian?
- Should hunting be allowed?

I imagine you can think of other questions which are likely to arouse strong emotions. The second step is to ask the participants to raise their hands (a) if they're strongly in favour and (b) if they're strongly against each idea. Then I pair them up: for and against.

Now for the third step. One person (the talker) spends two or three minutes explaining in the strongest possible terms why they're in favour of the idea. (They often have a good rant about it.) The second person's job is to listen carefully without speaking. I ask them to notice what's going on in their minds while the other person is talking.

After five minutes they switch roles. The talker becomes the listener and the listener becomes the talker.

During the discussion afterwards people describe how their minds were filled with thoughts about why they agreed or disagreed with the argument. Most find it hard to listen with an open mind. Instead, the mind keeps evaluating what's being said and/or formulating a response.

I encourage the participants to let go of their opinions and keep trying. If they do this, they usually find themselves simply listening to what the other person is saying.

If you use this exercise with friends or colleagues, ask them what they noticed when they listened with an open mind.

Participants often tell me:

- 'When I let go of my opinions, it becomes much easier to listen.'
- 'I get some new information.'
- 'Now I can see this issue from another point of view.'
- 'I found myself getting on better with the other person, instead of feeling irritated.'
- 'I don't feel quite so desperate to be right.'

LET GO OF CONCLUSIONS

Conclusions are closely related to stories, labels, judgements and opinions. We have a few experiences and then draw some conclusion. It could be 'Men are like this', 'Women are like that' or 'That's the way the world is'. We conclude that certain things work in certain ways.

It's OK to observe tendencies in human behaviour and the world around us, but conclusions are way more than that.

The Latin root of the verb *to conclude* means *to shut completely*. When we reach a conclusion about someone or something, we shut out all other possibilities. Then we misinterpret situations and miss out on opportunities. For example, if you conclude that everyone from a particular country, religion or ethnic group behaves in a certain way, you may treat someone unfairly. You may also miss out on a friendship or business opportunity.

Many of us have a list of conclusions that shape our lives, and we might not realize it's happening.

As the psychologist Carl Jung put it, 'when an inner situation is not made conscious, it happens outside, as fate.' If you keep returning to the present, you'll be much more aware of what's going on. You'll be much less likely to jump to conclusions.

Let go of conclusions

Turn an exercise book or pad of paper sideways (landscape way), so you can write horizontally on four pages. In the top left-hand corner of each page, write one of the following:

- The places you don't like.

- The kinds of people you don't like.

- The activities you avoid.

- The situations you avoid getting into.

On the left-hand side of each page, write down the events that have led you to this conclusion – one below another.

Now ask yourself the following questions and *write down* the answers:

- What's this conclusion costing me?

- What am I missing in life as a result of this?

- Now look at your list of conclusions again. How would you feel if you let go of them?

SEE THINGS AS THEY ARE

For several years I rented an apartment in a wealthy part of London and worked from home most of the time. When I first arrived it was common to see Porsches parked in the street. Over the years that followed the local car population gradually became more and more exotic – including Aston Martins, Ferraris, Lamborghinis and McLarens.

One day I was walking along when I saw a Ferrari parked on the side of the road. I stopped and looked at it more closely, and noticed that all kinds of thoughts were appearing in my mind. They weren't to do with not having a car – I have little interest in them. They were to do with money, or rather my lack of ready cash at the time. I felt frustrated and wondered if I would ever have plenty of money again.

I kept looking at the car, more and more carefully, without moving. After a while I realized I was looking at some metal painted red and some tyres made of black rubber. There was also a little yellow badge with a black horse rearing up on its hind legs – that was all.

Then I repeated the experiment with other objects. I saw a baby being pushed along in a buggy on the other side of the street. This provoked another flurry of thoughts and emotions. I was living on my own, while many of my friends were married with children. While these thoughts and emotions were appearing, I carried on looking at the objects themselves. There was a baby in a buggy. That was all.

Now it's your turn:

See things as they are

Whenever an object catches your attention, look at it more closely.

Do you see the object for what it is, or are you lost in thoughts about something else?

Whatever the thoughts may be, keep looking. Eventually they'll die down and you'll see the object for what it is.

In the next chapter I'll show you how to let go of the pain that *causes* these thoughts and emotions.

LET GO OF SHOULDS

Many of us feel we should *be* this or that, or *do* this or that, or *have* this or that. When things aren't the way we think they *should* be, we judge ourselves and feel bad. We may not even realize we're doing it.

Shake off your shoulds

Sit in a quiet place and make a list of all the things you feel you should be, do or have. Here are some ideas to help you get started:

- I should have done that.

- I shouldn't have done that.

- I should have a degree.

- I should be married.

- I should own my own home.

- I should be wealthy by now.

- I should be fitter.

- I should be X kilos lighter.

Getting your shoulds down on paper is a good start.

Now examine each one carefully. Where did it come from? Did someone say something which stuck in your mind? Did you pick it up from your friends, or did it come from someone in authority?

If you examine your shoulds carefully, they'll start to lose their power over you.

Now stand up, close your eyes and shake your body – particularly your hands and feet. Shake off all the shoulds.

Now bring your attention back to the present. Notice how you feel.

It can take a while to let go of your shoulds – keep shaking them off.

LET GO OF EXPECTATIONS

By definition, expectations aren't reality. They're just repetitive thoughts about how things should be. We get frustrated when people and situations don't meet our expectations. We keep resisting what is, and struggling against reality.

One afternoon I was having a conversation with a friend who knew I was stuck. He listened a lot and then said, 'What would you do if you were kind to yourself?' Then he disappeared for a few minutes to get another cup of coffee.

It was a sunny afternoon in early September and I gazed up at the buildings nearby. The first thing that came to mind was that I would take more photographs. Then it dawned on me: I would let go of my expectations.

Later that day I thought about the times in my life when I'd had few, if any, expectations. Exciting things had happened, often remarkably smoothly. Since then I'd accumulated all kinds of expectations, some of which hadn't been fulfilled. I realized the expectations were making me miserable, so I decided to let go of them – and immediately felt much better.

Let go of expectations

Take a blank sheet of paper and make a list of everything you expect to happen in your life.

Now turn over the page and write down how you expect people to behave. You can write down general standards of behaviour. You can also assign specific expectation(s) to each person.

This exercise may seem absurd – because it is. On the one hand there's reality, which is changing and evolving all the time. On the other hand there's the shopping list of expectations which your mind has drawn up and is now trying to impose on the world. They may be *legitimate* expectations, backed up by law or social convention, but they're still just *thoughts.* The mind is perpetually clashing with reality – guess which side is going to win.

You can tell people what you want them to do, and they may agree to do it. If they *don't* do it, you can take the appropriate action. At the same time, I recommend you *let go* of your expectations. *You're* the one who's going to suffer if you cling to them. Try this instead:

- Continue with your work and relationships in the normal way. Tell people what you want them to do. Sign contracts with them, if appropriate. Tell them what you're going to do, and then do it. But drop your expectations.

- Be present. Observe everything that happens moment by moment.

- Take action whenever it feels appropriate.

- How do you feel? Do you notice any difference in the way life unfolds?

When we let go of expectations, we allow people and situations to change. If someone you're working with doesn't do what they say they will, you can point it out to them. If they still don't do it, you may need to find someone else. There's no need to get stressed about it.

Things keep happening in the world which don't fit our expectations. Some people judge what's happening, get angry, label other people and so on. In the meantime, life keeps unfolding. If we let go of our expectations and judgements, we can stay calm and take the right action at the right time. Intuition will tell you what to do (as I'll explain in chapter 4).

THE IMPORTANCE OF NOT KNOWING

Our culture places a big emphasis on knowing. We accumulate knowledge from an early age and we're tested on it at school. People with vast amounts of general knowledge are celebrated in quiz shows. Not knowing is often seen as failure – so some people pretend to know things when they don't.

It's easy to overlook the fact that all knowledge is based on the past. Even language is based on the past, since words have conventional meanings agreed long ago. If we cling to what we think we know, we may fail to see what's happening now.

Sometimes we even try to know the future. Economic and financial forecasts are a good example. I once met an analyst who worked for a leading investment bank and specialized in the airline industry. Her job involved projecting airlines' earnings years into the future, based on various assumptions about the US dollar and the oil price. Shortly after she wrote one of her reports, the oil price halved. Everything changed.

If you see yourself as just a body/mind trying to get what it wants, then you may well feel a need to accumulate as much knowledge as possible – even if some of it's highly suspect. It will seem like your only hope of making a good decision.

As I said in the introduction, your brain and body are part of something far more intelligent. Once we realize this, our obsession with acquiring knowledge begins to subside.

Instead of trying to know everything, we analyse whatever information we have, and also use our intuition, which brings much better results. We don't need to know the future – we just need to tune in to what's happening now. Meditation helps us do this.

According to the *Tao Te Ching* (a Chinese classical text traditionally attributed to the sage Lao Tzu, who lived in the 6th century BCE, see page 193), 'Not-knowing is true knowledge. Presuming to know is a disease.' Admitting that you don't know may feel like weakness or failure at first, but it can lead to major breakthroughs. It helps us to let go of old ideas and concepts, and explore freely. We become open to new possibilities.

Sometimes it's best to ask a question and leave it open, instead of rushing to some conclusion.

LET GO OF THE NEED TO EXPLAIN EVERYTHING

When we experience something for which we have no explanation, it's tempting to invent one. This happens regularly with some of my friends. I've had many experiences which science can't explain. If I describe what happened, they leap in with 'scientific' explanations. They haven't had the experience themselves, but they have an instant explanation for *my* experience. Some of us don't need our friends to invent explanations – we do it for ourselves. We allow the mind to run riot.

It's better to…

KEEP AN OPEN MIND

If human beings were as rational as we like to think we are, we'd be open to information from any source, regardless of whether it fitted with our existing beliefs. Of course we would check to see if the new information was accurate, but being open-minded in the first place would help us to survive and prosper.

In reality, most of us suffer from *confirmation bias*: the tendency to look for information that confirms our beliefs, and ignore or fail to notice evidence that contradicts them, even if it's right in front of us. There's been a lot of research into confirmation bias. My friend Susanna Sällström Matthews used to teach at the University of Cambridge and is now an independent economist. She says the origins of confirmation bias aren't yet fully understood: 'Why are we biased against being open-minded? Why aren't we intrigued by evidence that contradicts our current beliefs, given the potential benefits from revising our beliefs to be a better match with our lives?'

There are ways of overcoming these biases and being more open-minded. The first step is to become *aware* of our confirmation bias.

Ironically, knowledge can make us *more* biased if we aren't careful. Once we acquire some knowledge we tend to notice evidence that's consistent with it, instead of noticing evidence that contradicts it. One technique Susanna recommends for overcoming confirmation bias is to let go of thoughts about what you'd expect to find on the basis of your knowledge.

Another simple way to start overcoming confirmation bias is to read newspapers and websites whose editorial opinions are the opposite of yours.

Many of us are trapped in a bubble

We have a natural tendency to surround ourselves with people who agree with us, both on and offline. Then it's easy to fall into the trap of believing that *most people* think, feel and behave in the same way as our immediate circle.

Social media has taken this a big step further by creating *filter bubbles*. The algorithm in a website figures out the information you like to see based on what it knows about you (which may be a lot). It wants you to keep coming back, so it keeps showing you information you'll like, and avoids showing you information that you probably won't. In short, the information you see on social media is tailored to your preferences and prejudices.

You can accelerate this process by 'unfriending' anyone whose opinions you don't like. After a while, you'll see little or no information which conflicts with your beliefs. As a friend of mine said after a surprising referendum result, 'How can this have happened? I don't know anyone who voted that way!'

Escaping from your bubble will help you spot new opportunities

After business school I spent three months working for Mercury Asset Management, which was Europe's largest independent fund management firm. I noticed that some of the most successful fund managers read the 'tabloids' – the cheap, popular newspapers which have much larger circulations than the 'highbrow' press. Reading the tabloids helped the fund managers to discover what people outside of their bubble were thinking. It gave them a better understanding of what was happening in the world – and was likely to happen next.

Try looking outside your bubble

- Buy a newspaper or visit a news website that you don't normally look at. It's best to choose one that isn't aimed at people of your social background.

- When you meet someone whose opinion is different from yours, ask them lots of questions. Let go of your opinions and listen. Learn as much as you can about what they're saying and how they see things.

- Go to a part of your city or region that you haven't visited before (provided it's safe to do so). Walk around. Watch and listen. Talk to people.

- Travel by public transport whenever possible. Put your phone away. Be present and pay attention to everything around you.

- Breaking a few habits will help you to see a bigger picture. You may find yourself having new ideas and spotting new opportunities.

LET GO OF CONSPIRACY THEORIES

Some people *love* conspiracy theories. The mind assembles a story about what's going on – and then gets excited while it pieces together new information that appears to fit the story. Essentially, it's confirmation bias in another guise.

If you do this you're likely to shut out any information that doesn't fit your story. You won't see things as they are, and you may make decisions which you later regret. If you really want to understand what's happening, it's best to let go of your theories, including any conspiracy theories. Just watch and listen with an open mind.

DON'T CLING TO PLANS – LET THEM COME AND GO

Plans can be useful at times. For example:

- **Business plans**
- **Planning a holiday**
- **Family planning**
- **Plans for evacuating a building in the event of a fire.**

These are sensible activities with obvious benefits. But some of us become so anxious about the future that we try to plan everything.

It's better to be clear about your intention, but keep an open mind about how it's going to be realized. You can start with an initial plan, and then adapt it quickly as circumstances change. Successful entrepreneurs usually have a vision for the kind of business they want to build. They start with a plan, which they update in response to changes in the economy, technology and what their customers want. They may sell or close down one business and start another. They may change the way the business works completely. Some conventional retailers have closed down all their stores and only sell online. Some online retailers are opening stores.

Career plans can be very limiting. The more we let go, the more we discover our talents – and so do other people. In the meantime, the economy is changing fast. Technologies such as artificial intelligence will carry out tasks that were previously performed by humans in highly regarded professions.

I sometimes meet people who have fixed ideas about what they're going to do and how they're going to do it. When we cling to our plans in this way, we often prevent – or slow down – something much bigger and more exciting which is trying to happen in our lives.

There's nothing *wrong* with plans, but we create problems when we *cling* to them. We start trying to manipulate people and situations in order to *make* them happen. It's better to let go. Our brains are part of something far more intelligent. Wonderful things happen in unexpected ways if we keep up a steady effort and allow things to fall into place.

The thing you decide *not* to do may happen anyway

The University Library in Cambridge holds several million books. When I first went there as a student I felt overwhelmed. Writing books seemed pointless to me, so I decided not to do it. You're now reading my fifth book, and the third to be published commercially – so what happened?

The short answer is that I kept meeting people who were struggling with similar problems, and did my best to help them. Then I started writing as a way to save time and help more people more quickly. One book idea came after another. While I was writing I always had enough work to pay the bills, and enough free time to complete the next book. I didn't plan it that way – it just happened.

GRATITUDE WILL HELP YOU FLOW WITH LIFE

Most of us have mental habits which help to keep us stuck. One of them is the habit of complaining. We can start getting rid of it by looking for things that make us feel grateful.

Instead of worrying about what's *going* to happen or what has happened, it's better to be grateful for what's *happening now*. (I'm going to use the words *gratitude* and *appreciation* interchangeably.)

My girlfriend at university was from Latin America. She'd grown up during a conflict in which tens of thousands of people disappeared, including some of her sister's friends. For a while my girlfriend was driven to school by a different route each day, with guns hidden under a blanket on the back seat of the car.

When I met her parents, I was struck by the way they appreciated things, whether it was a daffodil or a place they'd visited. At first it seemed like escapism to me. Surely they'd seen the poverty and conflict where they lived in Latin America? I'd grown up on a diet of economic and social gloom served up by Radio 4 every morning at breakfast time, but none of my friends had been kidnapped or murdered.

Years later, I began to understand how powerful her parents' attitude was. Whether they did it consciously or not, they kept appreciating every situation in which they found themselves. Everything else faded into the background. They'd married young and her father had worked his way up to become chairman of a large company. They now had children and several grandchildren. Appreciation worked for them.

If you think about people you know well, you may notice that some are continuously grateful for what's happening in their lives, while others keep focusing on what they think is missing. Some people flow with life, while others fight it. What would you rather do?

When I was 20 I had a habit of focusing on whatever I *didn't like* about a particular person or situation. Then I met people who focused on what they *appreciated*.

How to practise gratitude

Last thing at night, take a pen and a piece of paper, and write down everything you appreciate most about today. *Exclude* anything that's happened before today or that might happen in the future. This exercise is purely about today. Here are some examples:

- What you had for lunch or dinner.

- Someone's positive reaction to the work you did for them.

- A conversation you had with a friend.

- The weather.

- Some money you received.

- The project(s) you're working on.

- A new experience you had today.

- Something you learned.

- Something you created.

- Something that made you laugh.

- Something interesting that you saw on television or read about in the news.

Once you've finished, go to bed. Notice how you feel.

Notice how you feel when you wake up in the morning.

When I started practising this exercise, I noticed that I felt pretty good before I went to sleep. I used to feel a bit down in the mornings, but now I woke up feeling good too. The way I felt about things was gradually changing.

This exercise is based on facts – things that have already happened. All we're doing is changing what we focus on. Once we do that, we feel better and our lives begin to change.

Having learned this exercise, I started experimenting on my friends, as usual. One day, I had lunch with an old friend who had a habit of complaining – which often left me feeling negative.

When she asked what I was up to I told her about my latest experiments, including the gratitude exercise. I explained to her how it worked and then we went for a walk, and ended up at a street market. She bought a notebook from one of the stands, but I didn't think anything of it.

Two days later she sent me an email that was much more positive than usual. The gratitude exercise was working. Since then she's complained far less and has become more humorous. I've never seen anyone change so quickly.

Some people do this exercise before they go to bed, and again when they wake up. Both times are good, because the mind is relatively still, which makes it easier to let go of our mental habits. I recommend that you do this exercise for at least 21 days. You will then start noticing yourself feeling grateful at frequent intervals.

Don't count your blessings

Many of us have been taught to 'count our blessings', but we may then start to believe that what we've accumulated is 'ours'. We cling to it and become afraid of losing it. You may be wondering what the difference is between being grateful and counting blessings. Essentially:

- **Gratitude happens in the moment. You enjoy an experience and let it go.**
- **When you count your blessings, you label something as 'yours'. It could be a person, a physical possession, your reputation, some money...**

It's better to enjoy each experience, be grateful for it and let it go. For example, you might have a house in a nice neighbourhood, a loving family and lots of money. Any of them could disappear tomorrow. It's better to be grateful for each experience in the moment. It could be a smile from a child or a cup of tea on the lawn in the sunshine. Enjoy each experience and let it go.

B K S Iyengar was the founder of the style of yoga known as Iyengar yoga. In his book *Light on Life* he wrote that 'the correct attitude to our "possessions" is gratitude not ownership'.

Here's an exercise from the Zen tradition:

Imagine giving everything away

- When you wake up, lie still in bed for a few minutes.

- Think of your possessions and imagine yourself giving them away, one by one, starting with those you value the most.

- Once you've mentally given everything away, get up and carry on with your day as usual.

- Do this for several days in succession.

- How do you feel?

When I did this exercise I soon felt lighter and more relaxed. I also felt grateful for physical objects while I was using them, but I didn't feel so attached to them. I was still aware of how much money I had, but I no longer felt defined by it.

You're much more than anything you could ever possess.

Appreciate what's happening – and let it go

When we're consciously grateful once or twice a day, it spills over into the rest of our lives. We start to appreciate everything. Try this:

Be grateful in the present moment

Notice the temperature in the room where you're sitting. Notice the ground beneath your feet while you're walking around. Notice the sounds, colours and textures. Pay attention to what people are saying as well as how they say it.

Appreciate the air as it flows in and out of your body. Notice the weather, and the temperature of the air against your skin – and appreciate them.

Appreciate the food you're eating, the people you're meeting, the ideas you're sharing and the work you're doing. (If you have no work right now, you can appreciate the opportunity to reflect, meet new people and try new things.) Be grateful for any money you receive.

If you're delayed, pay attention to how you feel about it. Notice the sensations within your body, which may include tension or irritation. Appreciate the opportunity to observe what's going on in your mind, in your body and all around you. Be grateful for the lessons you're learning.

At one point it was taking me a while to switch from thinking about what was missing in my life to appreciating what was already happening – so I used an old trick to speed things up.

I wrote the word 'Appreciate!' in big, black letters on several fluorescent Post-it Notes. Then I stuck them in various places, including on my desk, the mirror above the sink and the door of the refrigerator.

If you keep appreciating, you'll start to feel different. Gratitude makes us feel light. You can even be grateful when things don't go the way you wanted. Life is pushing you to let go, which will bring you much more fulfilment. As Swamiji puts it, 'Everything is auspicious.'

Other people can help you see things in new ways

A friend of mine grew up in a war-torn country. When she came to the UK she noticed that people complained about trains being dirty and late. She was grateful that there were trains.

Appreciation will improve your relationships

Many of us have tried to fix other people – it doesn't work. When we focus on what we don't like, we usually get more of it. On the other hand, if we focus on what we appreciate in other people it can transform our relationships.

I'm not talking about flattery. I'm talking about looking for what we appreciate in people and then focusing on that. It helps them to feel good about themselves and to flourish.

Be grateful for your talents, intelligence and energy – and your ability to work hard

You may feel you've 'earned' what you have through your intelligence and hard work. You may also see yourself as talented, but where did all of this come from? Weren't you given your talents, your intelligence and your ability to work hard? In reality we've been given everything, so we can be grateful for it.

Gratitude puts you in tune with Existence

When we're grateful, we're in tune with everyone and everything. Things happen much more easily. This will become progressively clearer in the remaining chapters.

SUMMARY

- Thoughts about the past and worries about the future can keep us stuck and stop things from happening.

- You can let them go and create space for new things to happen.

- Let go of comparisons and thoughts about the past. Focus on what's happening now.

- Let go of your stories. Sometimes they just melt away if we look at them closely.

- Examine the labels you've applied to yourself and other people. Are they accurate 100 per cent of the time? What are all these labels costing you?

- Let go of judgements.

- Listen to new points of view. Let go of the need to be right.

- Make a list of all the things you feel you should be, do or have. Examine each one closely – where did it come from? Now stand up, close your eyes and shake off all your 'shoulds'.

- Your expectations of yourself and others are also just thoughts. Let go of them. Be present and observe.

- Follow your intuition. Take action where necessary.

- Let go of the need to know and explain everything. Keep an open mind.

- Read newspapers and websites you wouldn't normally look at. Ask questions of people whose opinion is different to yours. Go to new places and pay attention to everything around you.

- Don't cling to plans – let them come and go.

- Gratitude will put you in tune with Existence.

- Practise gratitude before bed – write down everything you appreciate most about things that happened today.

- Pay attention and appreciate everything around you.

- Looking for things to appreciate in other people will transform your relationships.

3

LET GO OF THE PAIN
THAT RUNS YOUR LIFE

Now it's time for the second step in the three-step process:

1. Let go of thoughts
2. Let go of pain
3. Let go completely.

In the last chapter I talked about observing thoughts and letting go of them. Now it's time to go deeper and consider the pain which perpetuates streams of negative thoughts.

WE TRY TO AVOID FEELING BAD

Every now and then we feel bad about something that's happening, or anxious about something that may or may not happen. Here are some examples:

- Someone close to you is seriously ill and may die.
- You have no job, no money, or both.
- You're afraid of something that might happen.
- Something you've wanted to happen for a long time still hasn't happened.
- Something you didn't want to happen has happened.

When we feel bad, many of us try to avoid it by doing one or more of the following:

- We suppress the feeling and try to focus on something positive. This usually doesn't work. We still feel bad at frequent intervals.
- We try to escape the feeling by taking lots of action. This may appear to work for a while, particularly if the action is directed at what we perceive to be the source of the

problem. We tell ourselves, 'At least I'm *doing something* about it!' – but we still feel bad inside. Other people pick up on our negative emotions, so our actions usually don't achieve very much.

PAIN FROM THE PAST

We allow pain from the past to run our lives

Negative thoughts and emotions vary from one person to another. This is because each of us has a particular set of painful experiences – from early childhood onwards – from which we've drawn negative conclusions about ourselves, other people and life.

If we keep drawing the same conclusions, they can become unconscious *thought patterns* which begin to run our lives – with negative results.

Pain from the past keeps reappearing

We've all had painful experiences, from early childhood onwards. The pain reappears at the most inconvenient times. It's like holding a football deep underwater. If you lose your grip, it rushes to the surface and leaps out of the water.

You've probably had the experience of talking to someone about something relatively minor and they reacted out of all proportion. Whatever you said triggered pain from the past which rushed to the surface.

Some of us like to focus on what we see as the positive aspects of our lives. We're glass-half-full people who don't dwell on the negatives. You can be as positive as you like – those painful experiences that you've suppressed will still come back up. It may be a sense that things aren't quite right – or something more dramatic that causes you to erupt in anger or sink into depression.

It's time to revisit the past

If you want to remove the pain that runs your life, you have to take a close look at your past. The pain from the past may be stored in your body. (I often ask people to think of the most traumatic event in their lives – without telling me *what* it is. In 99 per cent of cases, they can immediately locate the pain in their bodies.)

It's very likely that you've already had some experience of letting go of this pain. It could have been a bereavement or the end of a relationship. Here's a personal example:

Ever since my dad died I've kept a photo of him – taken a couple of months before – in my living room. In the photo it's a sunny day in the orchard at the bottom of my parents' garden. He's sitting in his wheelchair while I'm picking apples and passing them down to him. Despite his multiple sclerosis he's fooling around. In one hand he's holding a homemade apple-picking device consisting of a long stick with the top half of a plastic bottle lashed onto one end. He's talking into it while holding an apple to his ear, pretending it's an old-fashioned telephone.

In the first few weeks after he died, I would cry most times when I saw the photo. In neuro-linguistic programming (NLP), this is known as an *anchor* – an external stimulus, in this case a photograph – which triggers an internal response. I knew that anchors could become weaker and sometimes disappear altogether, so I kept the photo in my living room and looked at it several times a day. I allowed myself to feel the grief, which gradually became less painful. That was several years ago. These days when I look at the photo I usually feel happy. I appreciate my dad and the time we spent together.

Can you think of a time when you embraced negative emotions and gradually let go of them? There's no right or wrong answer, but it's nice to know your starting point.

How to let go of pain from the past

I've attended several programmes run by Swamiji on his ashram and elsewhere in India. He talks about *pain patterns*, which are mental impressions or psychological imprints. Pain patterns shape our lives even when we aren't fully conscious of them.

Another word for these pain patterns is *incompletions*, which he defines as 'incidents, memories and wrong cognitions from the past that are occupying the present and are affecting our future'.

Incompletions make us feel powerless. All our incompletions are based on suppressed emotions, which carry on ruling our lives for decades – unless we take specific action to get rid of them. Here are a couple of examples:

- **A schoolteacher asks a class of five-year-old children a question. A girl raises her hand to answer it, but she gets it wrong. All her classmates laugh at her, and she feels ashamed.**

- Fast-forward 20 years: this 25-year-old businesswoman is doing very well in her career but is afraid of public speaking. Every time she's asked to make a presentation to an audience, she's overwhelmed by negative thoughts. 'What if I mess this up?', 'People will laugh at me' and so on. She avoids public speaking as much as possible, and her career suffers as a result. An experience at the age of five creates a pain pattern which is still running her life two decades later.

- A four-year-old boy visits New York City for the first time, with his parents. They're walking along the platform when a train arrives at the station, slowing down as it passes them. Suddenly there's shouting and screaming up ahead. Someone has committed suicide by jumping on to the tracks right in front of the train. The boy can't see exactly what's happening, but the adults around him are pushing and shoving, trying either to get closer or to get away from the whole thing. The police show up. The boy is afraid of being crushed by the mob. This incident leaves such a strong impression that even into his 30s, this man still avoids train journeys. Whenever he's in a crowd he starts to panic.

The technique Swamiji teaches for letting go of pain patterns is called *completion*.

Note: If the exercises included in this book bring up memories that feel too painful to deal with by yourself, please do seek professional help, either through your general practitioner or a professional therapist.

COMPLETION

Completion – re-live to relieve

The first and most important step is to *decide* that you're going to let go of the pain patterns that are holding you back. Then you make a list of the incidents that caused you pain in the past. These incidents could have occurred in any area of your life at any time from early childhood onwards.

Sit in front of a mirror. Connect with yourself by looking into your eyes. Re-live each incident – at least five times – by talking aloud to the person in the mirror. This technique is known as *re-live to relieve*. Complete with each incident over a period of 20 minutes.

Please note that you don't *recall* the incident – you *re-live* it. If something painful happened when you were five years old, become five years old again, with the way you saw things at that age – not the way you see things now. The aim is to experience everything as a five-year-old, and to allow all the feelings to come up.

(If you don't have a mirror to hand, you can simply close your eyes, look inward and re-live the experience.)

This is what Swamiji says on the subject:

'When we intensely re-live the situation where we faced an incompletion, the intense conscious focus will help us to relieve the incompletion. Relive every suffering and suffocation that makes you feel you are not yet complete, which makes you feel you cannot manifest the life you want.'

Here's what I said when I practised this exercise:

'I'm five years old and my mum is taking me to a new school in a new city for the first time. She's holding my hand as we walk through the gates. The sun is shining and there's lots and lots of tarmac: the path and then an enormous playground with lots of children screaming and shouting. Now I'm in the classroom and the teacher is talking to us – a big group of boys and girls. I don't know any of them. She says we're going to leave the classroom and sit on the grass outside. She says "classroom" and "grass" differently to the way we say it at home. So do the other children. After I say something, one of the boys calls me a rude name. I feel very upset. Why are people laughing at me?'

When I first tried it, I felt a bit odd sitting in an ashram in India talking to myself in a mirror. But I soon realized it was working, which inspired me to continue. Once I'd re-lived each negative experience five or six times, I started getting bored with my story and it began to lose its power over me. Some of the most painful memories required several sessions over a few days, but they gradually bothered me less and less.

You can use completion to let go of fears

Most of us are afraid of something. It could be spiders, ill health or losing our job. Some fears are rational and help us survive, but in many cases they come from negative experiences which may never be repeated.

Once we identify those negative experiences we can remove the pain patterns they've created. Then we can stop worrying about the future and live our lives to the full. This is how my friend Halle got over her fear of flying:

I was flying back to London after visiting my mother in the US when it dawned on me that the 6mg of melatonin I'd taken wasn't working. I was wide awake, listening to the engines on a seven-hour flight. There was also turbulence, which made my stomach sink. Having been introduced to the completion exercise, I decided to give it a try. It was time I confronted my phobias of heights and of flying. I'd had these fears as long as I could remember. Going to an amusement park was not an option for me.

When I started to do the exercise, locating the source of pain wasn't difficult. It was a churning pain in my stomach. As I felt it, a painful episode when I was young emerged. There was a building my mum said was downright risky and a friend of mine she always disapproved of for being too spoilt and unruly. My friend used to come up with daring ideas during playtime. We would climb onto the roof, six floors up. The roof was shaped like a ski slope, with a flat piece at the bottom, followed by a six-storey drop. We would climb up the slope and slide down again to the flat part. If either of us had overshot we would have died.

We probably climbed up there a couple of times, and I knew it was far too dangerous to play there, but I never mentioned it to my parents. I felt guilty. At the same time I didn't want to lose my friend. It was a relief when her family were relocated and I never saw her again. Both our lives could have ended in tragedy.

During this exercise I realized that my phobias stemmed from that time. The two phobias were very much connected and it felt like a heavy stone was being lifted off me. When I tried re-living the episode for the first time, it was so painful my body trembled. Then it got easier on the third try.

On my fifth try, I felt something heavy lifting off me. I felt like a bird flying, as though I'd healed my broken wing. After that I recalled the incident again and felt no pain at all.

A few weeks later Halle flew from Norway to the US via London. The flight was free from pain and fear, on the way there and on the way back. On the overnight flight back to London she slept well for the first time in years.

How about you? What are you afraid of *now*, based on something that happened years ago?

You can apply this technique to any fear. For example, many of us are afraid of being rejected. This is what you can do to let go of it:

1. Turn inwards. Locate the fear in your body.

2. Go back as far as you can remember to the first time you felt rejected. It may have been in your early childhood.

3. Now become that age again. Re-live the experience from beginning to end. Allow anything to well up inside you, including emotions, thoughts, images, smells, anxiety, sensations, discomfort, agitation, pain – or any feeling of powerlessness.

4. Do this over and over again, in several sessions if you wish.

If you persist with this exercise, your fear of rejection will diminish and start losing its grip on you. You may even find it hard to remember what you used to be so agitated about.

Practise completion

Take a blank sheet of paper and write down a description of everything you're afraid of.

Go back and identify the original incident that led to this fear.

Use the completion exercise to re-live each experience until it loses its power over you. (This may require several sessions.)

Your pain patterns started very early in your life

We can usually trace the pain that runs our lives to a particular experience in early childhood. In my case, it suddenly became clear during a free webinar that Swamiji gave from India while I was sitting at home in London. This is what happened:

My parents were both from southern England, where I was born. When I was four we moved less than two hours' drive northwards, from Hertford to Leicester – now famous for the discovery of King Richard III's skeleton beneath a car park.

Although we hadn't moved very far, the local accent was different and it really struck me on my first day at school at the age of five. Unsurprisingly, I spoke with the same accent as my parents.

At that time, most of the presenters on BBC television spoke the same way as I did. But most of my young classmates had Leicester accents, and they made fun of me. It may sound absurd, but I chose my accent at the age of five. Faced with rejection at school I decided to carry on speaking like my parents and the people on the BBC. In the meantime, I felt *unacceptable*.

This mindset stayed with me for decades. Whenever I joined a new group of people I always found myself on the fringe of it. *I am unacceptable* was the pain pattern that had taken hold of me.

There's a gap between your inner image and your outer image

In my previous book, *Brand You* (with David Royston-Lee), we said that your personal brand should be like a tall building: visible from miles away. Many of us present a shiny exterior to the outside world, but the inside of the building is not like that at all. Imagine that your building has an atrium containing a fast-growing weed that quickly blocks out all the light. This enormous weed is a good analogy for a pain pattern from your early childhood. It gives rise to your *inner image*, which is the way you see yourself.

The gap between my inner image and my outer image became obvious during my first visit to Swamiji's ashram. There were 54 of us on the course and he told us how to identify our inner image (or self-image) and our outer image – the one we show to others.

The experience of being rejected by my five-year-old classmates had left me with a feeling that *I was unacceptable*. That was my inner image. My outer image was easy to identify: 'I'm clever and friendly'. For the next couple of hours, all 54 of us walked around the room introducing ourselves to each other. I told each person, 'My name's John. I'm unacceptable, but for you I'm clever and friendly.' Telling this story to one person after another highlighted the mismatch between the way I saw myself and the way I wanted other people to see me. (Of course, throughout my life some people had seen straight through the outer image to the inner image and realized that I didn't accept myself as I was.) I realized that this story had been shaping my life for decades.

Start discovering your inner image

I hope you can see from my example how your inner image – based on pain in the distant past – can shape your life. Your inner image consists of your thoughts and feelings about yourself – the stories you tell yourself about *you*.

Most of us aren't fully aware of what's going on. In chapter 2 (see page 64) I asked you to write down the answers to several questions, including the following:

- What's the story you tell about yourself?

- What are the beliefs underlying your story?

Your answers to these two questions will be a big help in discovering your inner image.

Sit quietly on your own with a pen and a blank sheet of paper. Write down what you believe about yourself and how you feel about yourself. Write down all your thoughts and feelings – whatever comes to mind, without holding back.

You're the only person who's going to see this, so write down how you really feel.

In case your mind has gone blank, I'll give you some common examples to help you get started:

- I'm not good enough.

- I'm not acceptable.

- I'm not lovable.

- I'm a failure.

- I haven't fulfilled my potential.

A lot of what you write may be negative and bring up strong emotions.

Once we get our beliefs and feelings about ourselves down on paper, we can take a good look at them. Can you see any connection between what you've just written and what's happening in your life?

Now, turn back to the completion exercise on page 105. Identify the incident when you first started believing this about yourself. Keep re-living that early, painful experience until the pain melts away.

Completion helps to empty the mind of painful thoughts

When I returned to London I carried on practising completion every day. After a couple of weeks I suddenly noticed that I had fewer regrets about the past and was worrying less about the future. One day I was walking across the park to the office when I noticed that there were almost no thoughts. There was just sunshine, trees and grass – the colours seemed brighter than before, and I was present nearly all the time.

The blissful emptiness lasted for about 24 hours. Then I had a conversation with someone about politics and the state of the economy. Some of the old, negative thoughts began to creep back in. Fortunately, I only had to do the completion exercise a few times to return to that feeling of infinite space.

Continuous completion will liberate you

The completion technique I've described in this chapter involves sitting down for a few minutes (ideally 20 minutes) at a time to re-live the experience which is causing pain, agitation or disturbance in you. Once you've done that and experienced the results, I encourage you to practise completion regularly throughout the day. Every time you have a painful experience, make sure you don't suppress it (thereby storing it inside you), or try to deflect it in some way. Please do this instead:

- **Turn inwards**
- **Find the pain, agitation or discomfort in your body**
- **Go back and find the original incident – when you first began to feel this way**
- **Re-live that experience exactly as it happened, from beginning to end.**

For example:

- **You get fired from your job and feel angry, frustrated or depressed. These are all powerless emotions. Now look back over your life and identify the first time you felt powerless in this way. Now re-live that experience of powerlessness. Allow everything to come out as you do so. Once you've completed that experience in the distant past, you'll feel more powerful. This will help you get a new job much more quickly.**

- Someone swears at you on the train, so you feel angry, insulted or humiliated. These are all powerless emotions. Again, look back over your life and identify the first time you felt powerless in this way. Now re-live that first experience of powerlessness. Allow everything to come out as you do so. Once you've completed the experience in the distant past, you'll feel powerful. Now you can be confident and at ease with everyone else you meet.

In each case, you turn inwards, find the original incident which is causing the disturbance – and complete it. You complete the experience by re-living it from beginning to end. *Re-live to relieve.*

The pain, suffering or discomfort will gradually dissipate, either in one session or in several sessions – depending on the intensity with which you re-live it. The more intensely you do so, the more you'll experience yourself as consciousness, which is bliss. You may also feel love, compassion, creativity – all apparently out of nowhere. They *are* coming from nowhere. They arise from pure consciousness and then find expression in you and in the world around you.

If you keep doing this, you'll find that your personal and professional relationships all become more harmonious. Things will happen much more easily than before. Your life will change for the better.

Turning inwards and feeling the pain runs counter to our cultural conditioning. So many of us have been told to 'focus on the positive' and 'keep smiling'. We then *suppress* negative thoughts and emotions, which keep rumbling around inside us and ruling our lives. As I mentioned earlier, all our pain patterns are based on suppressed emotions.

If *suppression* were an Olympic sport, the England men's team would surely win medals. Our prowess in suppressing emotions and pain patterns has formed the basis of comic characters ranging from Basil Fawlty to Mr Bean and beyond.

Another popular alternative to suppression is *analysis*. During clinical depression in my mid-20s, I experienced Freudian psychoanalysis (the classic technique of lying on a couch talking aloud to a man with a white beard). After many sessions over the course of a year, I'd told lots of stories and we'd identified lots of problems – but we hadn't solved *any* of them. To put it crudely, analysing my sh*t didn't help much. What really made a difference was flushing it away – using the completion technique (see page 105).

Deciding to complete is more than 80 per cent of the task. Essentially, we have a choice: we can either carry on living with our pain patterns and strengthening them, or we can get rid of them. Getting rid of them simply requires us to re-live each original experience fully, without running away from it, suppressing it or analysing it.

With a bit of practice, completion becomes automatic. It's a bit like an engine running in the background while you go about your daily activities. It may judder to a halt now and then, so you have to intervene and restart it. Completion requires us to become *conscious* of what's going on inside us, so we can deal with it. You have a negative thought or emotion, so you face it. You feel it. You hear yourself out, with no judgements.

When we complete each experience in this way, we no longer store pain in our system. We feel light and free. It's much easier to make things happen.

We can still recall what happened if we need to, but painful events in the past lose their emotional charge and no longer shape our lives. For me, episodes such as clinical depression and my father's death are like books in a library. I can fetch a book and open it whenever I want to, but it doesn't rule my life.

Completion helps us to be grateful

Once we face and complete the pain patterns which have been running our lives, we naturally feel grateful for everything that's happening, moment by moment. We tune into Existence and the things we want to happen start happening much more easily.

Completion helps us to let go of regret

We regret the past because we've stored the pain which continues to generate hundreds or thousands of negative thoughts. Once we complete with the pain, it stops generating thoughts. We can still go back and find the event in our memories – like finding that book in a library – but the stream of regretful thoughts dies down.

Completion will improve your relationships

When you change, the people around you change. So do the situations in which you find yourself. Romantic relationships are a good example. Many of us have experienced the following:

- **You fall in love with someone – and it's blissful at first.**
- **Sooner or later your mind starts labelling aspects of the person or the relationship as *problems*, which feel painful and 'need to be solved'.**
- **You then start trying to fix the person or the relationship, so you can feel good again.**

This approach doesn't work – it's even worse if both of you try to fix each other. Fortunately, there's an alternative approach, which you can apply right now:

- **Stop trying to fix the other person. Stop analysing the relationship. Both are a reflection of you.**
- **Turn inwards and work on yourself. Identify each pain pattern as it comes up – and complete it.**
- **Do this continuously.**

The more you complete your pain patterns, the better you'll feel and the more you'll love your partner – and everyone else.

You may recall what I said in chapter 1: after I learned to be present and let go, my mum became calmer. The same thing happens with completion. As soon as you complete and remove a pain pattern in yourself, it affects everyone around you. All your relationships will improve.

Don't become his or her psychotherapist

When you're getting to know a potential partner, it's easy to fall into the trap of trying to solve their problems. Men are particularly prone to this. Then we wonder why we end up in the 'friend zone' instead of a romantic relationship.

You may recall what I said about anchors (as described in NLP) earlier in this chapter (see page 102). If you spend lots of time analysing the other person's problems that are causing them pain, you'll establish an anchor in their minds which connects you with pain. Every time they think of you, they'll feel pain!

We all want to be with people who make us feel good. This is particularly important in a romantic relationship. If you do the exercises in this book, you'll be much happier than before, so people will want to be with you. Of course you should listen carefully when someone tells you about a painful experience, or some pain they're feeling. You can empathize and acknowledge what they've said, but don't analyse them or try to fix them.

WHAT ABOUT THE PEOPLE YOU FIND REALLY ANNOYING?

The problems we have with other people tend to follow a pattern. In other words, we have the same or a similar problem with different people, at different times and in different places. It could be something that happens in one job after another, one business after another or one relationship after another.

The people you find really annoying

Take a blank sheet of paper. On the left-hand side, make a list of the people you find most annoying. Please include both individuals and types of people. Write down as many as you can. Start with friends and family members. Then think about colleagues, past and present. What about people you know through sport and other leisure activities? Now think about people you've seen on television or online, or read about. Are there famous people – or particular types of people – who you find annoying? Please write down as many as possible. The more data you have to work with, the better.

To the right of each name on the list, write down what you find most annoying about them.

You'll end up with something like this:

Who I find most annoying	What I find most annoying about them
Jack	....
Jill	....
Deepika	....
Hieronymus	....
And so on	....

Do you keep having similar problems with different people? What are the patterns in your relationships? Write them down. This will help you to make a valuable discovery, as I'll explain.

Eventually, some of us realize that *we're* the common factor in all these situations. We can change job, find a new partner or emigrate, but the same things keep happening.

For years I had problems with judgemental people who kept showing up in my life. At work I seemed to be surrounded by judgemental colleagues. I also had two relationships with women who were highly judgemental, which I found entertaining for a while, but ultimately exhausting. Instead of being present and enjoying life, I had to keep justifying myself.

The people you find annoying have a message for you

You may be shocked to hear me say this, but the things you find annoying in other people are a reflection of *you*.

IT'S TIME TO LOOK AT YOUR SHADOW

The *shadow* is a term coined by Carl Jung. Another word for it is the *dark side*. It contains anything you've failed to accept about yourself, which you then project – unconsciously – onto other people. In the meantime you keep having the same problems with other people, over and over again.

The way to understand your shadow is to look at the people who annoy you most – hence the last exercise. What annoys you about them is something you've *suppressed* in yourself and *projected* onto them. Whatever it is, you'll keep seeing it in other people until you acknowledge it in yourself and embrace it. Then you'll start to become *whole*.

In my case, those judgemental colleagues and girlfriends were clues to what was happening. How had I projected being judgemental onto them? Then it dawned on me: *I* was judgemental, sometimes extremely so.

I'd denied that I was judgemental and had projected it onto other people. Judgemental people then kept appearing in my life to remind me. They would carry on doing so until I became whole.

Things had been difficult with my previous girlfriend since we'd split up. The next time I saw her, I told her I realized I'd been judgemental, just as she'd always insisted. 'Finally', she said. After that, the situation magically improved. She was far less judgemental, and fewer judgemental people showed up in my life.

Overweight men also wound me up – particularly men in their 40s and 50s. I kept bumping into them, sometimes literally. I couldn't figure out what was going on. Strangely, overweight women didn't bother me.

Then I realized: I'd been trying to lose three or four kilos for ages. I knew I had more energy when I was lighter and ran better, but I'd been fighting the fact that I was overweight, instead of embracing it. Hey presto! I was surrounded by overweight men, silently reminding me that I hadn't accepted being overweight.

I experimented with thinking about the subject differently. 'I'm overweight' didn't feel so good. I also tried, 'I'm heavier than I want to be'. That didn't feel great either. It implied that I didn't accept myself as I was – which obviously wasn't going to work.

Then I tried, 'I *can* be overweight'. That felt much better: it was something I was capable of being. I might or might not be overweight at any particular time.

Gradually, overweight men somehow appeared in my life less frequently. Maybe they were still there but I wasn't noticing them so much. Within a few weeks, people were commenting that my weight had fallen, even though I'd made no particular effort. (A possible explanation is that once I'd accepted every aspect of myself, I was more relaxed and less prone to 'stress eating' – consuming food in response to feelings, regardless of being hungry or not.)

My problems with judgemental people and overweight men went away once I became whole. As Carl Jung put it, 'Everything that irritates us about others can lead us to an understanding of ourselves.'

Our shadow includes judgements about ourselves which we've projected onto other people. Once we discover them, we can embrace them and let go of them – as I'll show with the shadow exercises on the following pages.

What if the people you find annoying do something you never do?

On one occasion I was running a workshop when a smiling, well-dressed woman in the audience told us about a 'vagabond' who'd muttered something while she was walking past him earlier that evening. When she stopped to hear what he was saying, he blew smoke in her face, which she found very annoying.

When I asked her if she smoked, she said no. When I asked what she found annoying about this incident, she said that smoking was harmful and could cause cancer. Then I asked her if she could think of times when she'd harmed people. She thought about it and said, 'I've harmed people sometimes with the words I've used. I've hurt others knowingly or unknowingly.'

It takes courage to look inside and face aspects of ourselves that we've suppressed, denied or simply failed to notice. Once we do this we can embrace them and become whole.

Integrate your shadow and become whole

In chapter 2, I asked you to write down your stories about *other people*. Here are the examples I gave:

- People are so rude.

- Everyone's out for themselves.

- They're all a bunch of show-offs.

- All politicians are liars.

Once you identify a story you tell about others, you can turn it into a question about you. For example:

- When have I been rude?

- When have I been selfish?

- When have I been a show-off?

- When have I lied?

Once you've identified the behaviour you've been denying in yourself, you can start to embrace it. For example:

- I can be rude.

- I can be selfish.

- Sometimes I show off.

- Sometimes I tell lies.

Please note that I'm not asking you to label yourself. You're just identifying things that you're capable of being and doing. If you embrace every aspect of yourself, you'll start to become whole.

BECOMING WHOLE

It's better to be whole than good

Trying to be good is stressful and tiring. If you decide you *mustn't* be judgemental, you'll find yourself constantly checking your thoughts and behaviour for any misdemeanour. You may also find yourself monitoring other people, in case *they* start judging anyone.

Relax. It's better to be whole than good. We can all be judgemental at times. What's the big deal? We can be anything. Let go and give yourself a break. The chaotic thoughts will continue to die down, making it much easier to be present and enjoy each moment.

Wholeness is (very) attractive

On the first page of the introduction, I asked you what you wanted to change in your life. Was a relationship on your list?

Many of us believe that a relationship will complete us or make us whole. We think something is missing in our lives and that someone else can make the bad feeling go away. Unfortunately, other people pick up on our negative feelings, which then scare them off.

It's better to accept every aspect of yourself. Then you'll feel good about yourself and other people will feel good around you. Relationships develop naturally when we no longer feel the need to fix ourselves and everyone around us.

Accept that you can be anything.

Integrating your shadow and becoming whole

When there's no one else around, try reading the following statements out loud:

- I can be clever

- I can be stupid

- I can be beautiful

- I can be ugly

- I can be fat

- I can be skinny

- I can be mean

- I can be generous

- I can be kind

- I can be unkind

- I can be old

- I can be youthful

- I can be lazy

- I can be energetic

- I can be fascinating

- I can be boring

- I can be rich

- I can be poor

- I can be patient

THE POWER OF LETTING GO

- I can be impatient

- I can be tidy

- I can be untidy

- I can be efficient

- I can waste time.

Do you get the idea? Once you realize that you can be anything, you start to become whole. You're no longer trying to be one thing and not another. You'll feel better about yourself – and other people will feel better around you.

Even people who want to pick a fight with you will find it much more difficult once you accept that you can be anything. Every now and then someone labels me on social media or in real life. I no longer feel any need to defend myself. My usual response is, 'You can label me in any way you wish.'

People who accept themselves as they are don't feel the need to hide qualities which some people may not like. Not everyone is attracted to them, but plenty of people are. If you want a romantic relationship, you only need to attract one person.

If you want a successful career, you don't need to attract everyone either. Just accept every aspect of yourself – then you'll feel better. As I explained in *Brand You*, you'll attract people who want what you do in the way that you do it.

Maybe you've been showing aspects of yourself which you think everyone will approve of, while hiding aspects which might turn some people off. The danger is that you won't appeal to *anyone*.

In Britain there's a well-known food spread made from yeast, called Marmite. (The Australian equivalent is Vegemite.) People either love or hate Marmite. If you want to appeal strongly to some people, you have to be prepared to scare some other people off. If you think about the most successful popstars, politicians and comedians, a lot of them are like Marmite.

Once you've accepted every aspect of yourself, you can decide which aspects you want to show to other people, and in which situations. For the first four years of my career in executive search, I was very selective about what I allowed colleagues and clients to see in me. They saw the hard-working, efficient consultant with shiny shoes who stayed calm and never got into fights. That helped me become a partner, but then I realized that I had to show more of myself in order to stand out in a crowded market and win business.

These days I'm much more open than I was in the early years. If a client or candidate talks to me about clinical depression, I tell them that I suffered and recovered from it in my mid-20s. Some people are surprised, which is itself surprising since clinical depression is so common. Some people are drawn to me. They or someone they know has had it too. I've opened up, so they open up, and we form a stronger bond.

Let go of the habit of judging yourself and others

In chapter 2 I said that if you judge you suffer. Many of us reserve our harshest judgements for ourselves. Once we accept every aspect of ourselves, it becomes much easier to drop this habit. What's the point of judging yourself if you can be anything?

Once you accept every aspect of yourself, you have nothing to project onto other people. You're much less likely to judge them. Letting go of judgements is good for you and everyone around you.

Other people may project their 'stuff' onto you

Next time someone judges you, consider the possibility that they're projecting aspects of themselves onto you. In other words, they're judging you for something they find unacceptable in themselves. You don't need to say anything about this – you can just notice it and let it go.

Now it's time to go deeper

If you've done the shadow exercises from page 122 onwards, you'll have discovered what you've been projecting onto other people. That's already a big help. You'll start to become whole.

Now we can go a level deeper and become whole *full stop*, using the completion technique. Here's a personal example, which combines the shadow exercises and the completion technique:

1. I notice that (a) I judge people who are overweight and (b) I label other people and their behaviour as unacceptable.

2. I do the shadow exercises and realize that (a) I feel uncomfortable about being overweight and (b) I find *myself* unacceptable in various ways. Now I know where those projections are coming from – I can see what I'm doing.

3. I look back over my life and figure out when these patterns started:

   (a) The first time I started putting on significant amounts

of weight was at the age of 26. I felt I was in the wrong job and couldn't see a way out. I felt stuck. Then I was diagnosed with clinical depression. I started eating quite a lot between meals, which made me feel better – for a short while at least. Then my weight started rising.

(b) It was my first day at school, at the age of five. The other children laughed at my accent, so I felt unacceptable.

4. Now that I know when the patterns started, I use the completion technique explained earlier in this chapter (page 105). I sit quietly on my own, become a depressed 26-year-old again and re-live the experience of feeling stuck. Then I go back even further and become the five-year-old on his first day at school. *I re-live to relieve.*

5. I keep doing this over and over again, in several sessions – as intensely as I can. I let go of the pain, discomfort, agitation etc.

6. I feel happy, light and free.

We're extremely unlikely to dig out all of our incompletions in one go, but at least we're looking in the right place. The shadow exercises can help us do this. Then we can dig deeper and deeper, to get rid of all the incompletions.

Now it's your turn

What are you projecting onto other people?

What are the pain patterns which are causing you to do this?

I invite you to complete them and let them go.

Keep looking inwards. Keep digging and completing.

SUMMARY

- Repetitive, negative thoughts are caused by deep-rooted pain which rules our lives.

- Sometimes we suppress pain and try to focus on something positive. We still feel bad at frequent intervals.

- At other times we try to escape the feeling by taking lots of action, but we still feel bad inside.

- Pain patterns or incompletions are based on suppressed emotions which can rule our lives for decades.

- The completion technique (page 105) allows you to re-live experiences and so relieve your pain patterns.

- We've all had a painful experience in early childhood which continues to shape our lives. This means that your inner image is different to the image you project to the world.

- You can discover your inner image using the exercise on page 111, and then complete the experience that led you to create that inner image.

- Continuous completion will help you experience yourself as consciousness. You'll experience love, compassion and creativity as if from nowhere. Your personal and professional relationships will become more harmonious.

- To understand your shadow, look at the people who annoy you. What annoys you about them is something you've suppressed in yourself and projected onto them.

- When you acknowledge and embrace this shadow part of you, you'll start to become whole. The exercise on pages 122–126 will help.

- Again, you can identify the pain patterns which have given rise to your shadow. Use the completion technique to re-live them and let them go.

4

SURRENDER AND TUNE
INTO SOMETHING FAR
MORE INTELLIGENT
THAN YOUR BRAIN

Just to recap, this is what we've covered in the first three chapters:

- How to be present
- How to let go of the thoughts which have been holding you back
- How to let go of the pain which has been ruling your life.

Now we've done the groundwork, we can move on to the really exciting bit, which is letting go completely. This is sometimes called *surrender*. I must warn you that surrender may seem paradoxical at first, but letting go completely is much more productive than trying to control everyone and everything. It also has the power to transform your life, so it's worth experiencing for yourself.

The best way for me to explain surrender is to tell you how to do it:

How to surrender

If you've done the exercises in chapters 2 and 3 you'll have started letting go of negative thoughts and emotions. Now it's time to let go completely. Forget about the past and the future. Forget about your goals, plans and expectations. Let go of all your memories. Drop all your thoughts about the present, including judgements, labels and expectations. Close your eyes and imagine yourself throwing them all away.

Now do whatever feels appropriate moment by moment. If you keep a to-do list, pick the item which needs your attention now and work on it.

Follow your intuition – do whatever feels right, moment by moment.

Let go of any thoughts about the outcome. Don't bother thinking about results. Just immerse yourself in whatever you're doing and enjoy it.

If we keep thinking about goals and action plans we're constantly pulled *away* from the present moment. The same thing happens if we keep thinking and talking about the past – it drags our attention away from the present.

When we surrender, we *fall into the present.* We let go of thoughts about the past and the future. Now you're tuning into what's really happening, instead of what your mind thinks *should* happen or *should have* happened. This enables big changes to occur.

When I surrendered I suddenly felt more relaxed. I began to notice my surroundings in more detail. Walking down the street where I'd lived for several years, I noticed for the first time that the houses at the end of the street had attic windows. Colours seemed a lot brighter.

I became much more productive, whether I was writing a document, organizing something or communicating. I also remembered things more easily now that my mind wasn't cluttered with thoughts about the future. These days, if I can't remember someone's name, I surrender and it usually comes to me in a short while.

I also found myself having conversations in which I focused on what people were saying without making any particular effort.

I had more energy and enjoyed life moment by moment, without any expectations. I felt grateful for everything that was happening.

I also had a strong feeling of love. (There's no other word for it.) I was less irritated by what I saw happening around me. Instead, I laughed more – including at myself.

SURRENDER YOUR WAY TO SUCCESS

For most of us, the word *surrender* goes against all our conditioning and the culture we've grown up in. (A friend of mine who enjoys military history said to me, 'I'm not big on surrender.') Maybe you'd like to think of surrender in another way. Surrender is like sky diving: scary at first but exhilarating once you get into it. Or imagine that you're clinging on to the bank of a river, and then you surrender and go with the flow of the water. It's easy: you travel great distances with hardly any effort, instead of fighting to remain stuck in the same place.

In this chapter, I'll show you what happens when we surrender to Existence: our lives change radically for the better. The reason is that we stop relying on our brains to figure everything out. Instead, we tune into something far more intelligent.

One way or another, life keeps pushing us to surrender. Just when we think we've got our act together, something happens that looks like a disaster. Months or years later – with the benefit of hindsight – we can see that it was exactly what was needed to destroy a bit more of the ego and make us let go. I surrendered because I *had* to. There was no other option.

How I began to surrender

I was living in Paris, running a business which had ground to a
halt. I'd run out of money and my relationship was coming to
an end. In the meantime I was feeling depressed and had
sciatica, which made it very difficult to walk. In short, nothing
in my life was working.

In the midst of all this I was reading a rather hopeful-sounding
novel called *A Rich Man's Secret*, in which the main character
did a simple exercise that involved 'returning to now'. I started
doing the same exercise and soon felt much better. (I later
discovered that I'd learned mindfulness without realizing it.)

Then I stood back from the situation and took a fresh look at
what was going on. For years I'd been trying to make things
happen by thinking a lot and working really hard. It had become
more and more stressful, and the situation had become worse
and worse.

The social scientist in me found this interesting. I was very well
qualified and had been working hard for years. Realistically, I
couldn't work any harder, but I was getting nowhere and felt
completely stuck. This suggested that I was doing something
fundamentally wrong. If I could figure out what it was and
change it, my life was likely to improve quickly.

It occurred to me to let go, so I did. I stopped making business
appointments and gave up trying to get people to do things.
Whenever I noticed that my attention had wandered, I brought
it gently back to the present moment. This was happening over
and over again each day, more and more frequently. I was able
to observe my thoughts and emotions, which helped me to
understand myself much better. This was when my intuition

switched on like a searchlight, as I mentioned in chapter 1.
I would just have a feeling about people I met and what I
should do next.

Having been to church and Sunday school between the ages of
five and fifteen, I was in the habit of praying. Many people pray
for certain things to happen in their lives. I just prayed to be
guided to the right job or business. Then I let go.

For a few years I'd been trying (and failing) to earn a
particular income, and now I began to explore other career
options. A couple of ideas occurred to me, one of which was
executive search, otherwise known as headhunting. I'd been
very interested in it when I was at business school, but at that
time I knew I lacked the intuition required to be any good
at evaluating people. Now that my intuition had become
much stronger, maybe it was time to take another look at
executive search.

A short while later, an advertisement appeared in the
recruitment section of *The Sunday Times*. A large executive
search firm was looking for consultants with the potential to
become partners. The salary on offer was more than the amount
I'd been trying and failing to earn for five years. (At this point
my income was zero.)

I replied to the advertisement and was invited for interview.
Over the next few weeks I met 16 partners in London and
Paris. Each interview lasted an hour, and many of them asked
the same questions. Knowing how to be present was a big
advantage. Before each interview I placed my attention on
my breath and then on each of my senses. This enabled me
to listen carefully for an hour at a time.

I also had some interviews with another global search firm. It was an obvious place for me to work because they employed lots of MBAs, including several from INSEAD where I'd studied, but they turned me down. At first I felt frustrated, but then I remembered to let go. I asked to be guided and kept returning to the present over and over again.

A few weeks later the first firm offered me a job, which I accepted. There was a base salary and a guaranteed bonus which meant that I was now earning significantly more than the amount I'd been striving for. Strangely, my goal became reality once I'd given up thinking and trying so hard. Instead, I'd returned to the present, asked to be guided and let go. Having been stuck for years, I'd suddenly made rapid progress.

Now for the weird bit. A few months after joining the firm, I stumbled on a memo from a senior member of staff, in which he said the firm had decided to recruit some new consultants just below partner level. He also described what the firm was looking for, listing five criteria.

It was uncanny: I matched all five. It was a perfect fit. In six months I'd gone from a failing business to the perfect job. After years of struggle and effort I'd reached my goal by letting go.

I had to hit rock bottom before I surrendered. Then my life changed rapidly for the better. What had seemed like a very painful experience turned out to be a blessing in disguise.

Please note that you *don't* have to wait for your life to become as difficult as mine was before you let go. You can start letting go right now, exactly where you are. If you do this, you'll avoid a lot of pain. Either we let go or life *pushes* us to let go. Some of us need a big push, but *you* don't have to be one of them.

You could argue that my experience in Paris and London wasn't statistically significant: it was just a one-off experience among many others. But it was highly significant for me. It changed my life. It also pointed me towards a new way of living, which I've followed ever since.

I've met many other people who've let go and allowed their lives to change rapidly for the better. I hope you'll be one of them.

Another example of surrender

This is what happened to a friend of mine:

> I used to run a considerable part of a global media agency, before going on to start my own media consulting company. In work, I was successful.

> Having a baby proved much more difficult. The medical examinations showed that neither my husband nor I could have a baby naturally, so we went for IVF. After four trials the baby still didn't come, so I decided to switch to another gynaecologist. He also carried out a general health examination which showed that I was sensitive to gluten, which can cause infertility – so I changed my diet.

> My fifth IVF process was scheduled for October. In the meantime, one of my best friends invited me to stay with her on the French Riviera. I love the sea and the sunshine, and doing nothing was the perfect vacation for me.

> I'm a terrible swimmer. I wanted to float gently in the water and keep my hair and eyes dry – but the sea kept

surging in big waves. I was getting stressed about going under the water, and was afraid of the huge waves which were coming at me. Eventually I realized that I had to change my approach – and follow the direction of the waves – if I was going to enjoy swimming.

This was a huge discovery for me. It dawned on me that I shouldn't fight against the huge waves, as they would always be stronger than me and push me under. I should just collaborate with them. Then maybe I would get what I wanted, rocking and swimming in the water.

We went ahead with the fifth IVF process in October, still wanting a baby but having some doubts. It was kind of, 'Let's see what happens.' I was very surprised when I was told that I was pregnant, and my daughter was born the following June.

In October the following year, a few months after we'd moved into a new flat, I had a feeling I might be pregnant again – I had the same strange way of breathing I'd experienced when my daughter was so tiny that the medical instruments couldn't detect her existence. A week later it turned out to be true. My son was conceived and born in the normal way, despite the medical diagnosis that my husband and I couldn't conceive naturally.

I'd already understood the concept of letting go intellectually, but I only learned to put it into practice once I'd experienced it physically in the sea.

As Swamijii puts it, 'Surrender is allowing Existence to happen through you.'

When you surrender you'll let go of the person in your stories

Remember the stories we talked about in chapter 2? All that stuff about not being good enough, being a winner, being a loser? The exercises you've done since then will help you let go of the stories which have been holding you back.

Now for another weird bit. When you surrender you let go of *both* the stories *and* the person who appears in them. S/he is just a story too.

When we're born we simply *are.* As small babies we have experiences, we laugh and we cry, but we don't yet have a story about ourselves as a person. That comes later.

Soon we're given a name, a mother tongue, a nationality and perhaps a religion. Over the years that follow, our parents, teachers, bosses and others keep telling us that John Purkiss or Frida Smith has been naughty or nice, has a great future (or not) and so on. It's one huge story, which is constantly being updated. By the time you're an adult, you've accumulated lots of episodes describing the adventures, achievements and suffering of John or Frida.

Eventually you may realize that the story of John or Frida is just a stream of thoughts. Your story may seem real enough – like watching a film – but it isn't. It's just a series of thoughts strung together. This is how my friend Susanna describes it:

> I find it immensely helpful letting go of thoughts about 'Susanna'. I had a beautiful experience the other day when my being just jumped off the bike to help a neighbour carry his bags to his house, with no

conscious thought in my head. It was a beautiful experience because in the past I would have observed what was happening and said to myself, 'He needs your help', but now it just happened.

PURE CONSCIOUSNESS

So what's the alternative? What if you *aren't* the person in the story? Who are you? The answer is that you simply *are*. You're consciousness. Thoughts, emotions and sensations appear and disappear within consciousness. It's like a film being projected onto a screen. You're the screen, not the film.

Once we realize that we're consciousness – and let go completely – it gives a tremendous feeling of space, in which there are infinite possibilities. Anything can be projected onto the screen.

Consciousness is there all the time – not just during deep meditation. In the introduction I gave you several examples of letting go. Here are three of them again. They all result in pure consciousness:

- You wake up naturally, without an alarm. For a moment or two – at least – there are no thoughts. Gradually, you begin to notice your surroundings. You wonder what time it is, and you think about breakfast. The thoughts have started up again, and may continue for the rest of the day.
- You're standing on top of a mountain – or on a clifftop – in front of a scene so beautiful that your mind falls still. Maybe the stillness only lasts for a few moments. Then the thoughts start up again: 'Should I take a

photo?', 'Who's that person over there?', 'This reminds me of that place I went to last year.'

- At the end of a yoga session you lie on your back in *shavasana* (corpse pose). Your whole body tingles and – for a second or two at least – there are no thoughts.

Have you experienced any of these situations – or anything similar? They're all examples of pure consciousness, otherwise known as pure being, pure awareness or pure presence. You *are*.

Here are three experiences described by friends of mine:

I was sailing across the Aurlandsfjord, not very far from Bergen in Norway. It was a beautiful sunny day, but windy and cold. I decided after a while to reach the ferry's bow where I could enjoy the best view. I stayed there for a while, hard to say for how long, but probably half an hour at least. I was very close to the boat's balustrade and the only things I could see were the water, the cliffs and the sky. The wind was covering up the external sounds; I could hear neither the crowd nor the boat. After minutes of deep contemplation – where various unorganized ideas were crossing my mind about life, the future, the hotdog I'd just eaten, etc. – I started all of a sudden disconnecting from all my thoughts. A strange overwhelming feeling of greatness, joy and silence took place. No other thoughts were competing. My mind was blank.

When I stood in front of Nasrid Palace in the Alhambra, I was so mesmerized by its beauty that my mind went blank for a second. It was the most beautiful 'thing' I'd ever seen in my life. The beauty moved me so much that I then felt tears in my eyes. When I got back to 'reality', I started to admire the architectural detail of the palace (the carving, the water fountain, etc.).

Floatation tanks are designed to give total relaxation to people who are able to 'let go'. Basically, a floatation tank is a very large bath filled with Epsom salts water raised to exactly body temperature, in a sound-proofed room with a lid placed on the tank to remove all light. The 'floater' gets into the bath and is told to relax, lying as still as possible, which is quite easy due to the supporting effect of the salt water. Then, the lid is placed on the tank and the experience begins.

Firstly, you become very aware of the sensory deprivation as this isn't a 'normal' state to be in – there's no light, no sound and you can't feel your body as it's suspended in the salt water at body temperature. It's at this point that some people panic and choose to leave the tank as it can be quite claustrophobic. But for those people who are able to 'let go' and relax, the results are quite extraordinary.

For me, the experience started with trying to comprehend what was happening…could I really not feel my arms…or my legs? All my senses were silent – no light, no sound, no feeling – this was quite unusual and amazing. I have no idea how long I was analysing the situation, but after only a short space of time, I suddenly wondered if I'd been sleeping. I was sure I was awake, but there was nothing going on in my head – all my brain energy had stopped and I'd lost all sense of time.

And then almost immediately after thinking this, I again wondered if I'd been sleeping…this time also taking a second to remember where I was. And then again…was I sleeping? Where was I? How long had it been? Hang on, was I sleeping? Without realizing it at the time, my mind was in a deeply relaxed state, jumping through layers of consciousness.

And then…suddenly the lid was being taken off the tank. Was it over? I had absolutely no idea how long it had been. I felt like I was waking up from a very deep sleep.

I got out of the tank and was told that my hour was up. I was amazed as I'd lost all sense of time. If someone had told me I'd been there for eight hours I would have believed them, but I would also have believed them if they'd told me it was eight minutes! What a strange feeling. And once I'd fully 'woken' up, I felt fantastic and very refreshed.

Letting go of the person in your stories is liberating and exciting

These glimpses of pure consciousness are profound. When there are no thoughts, there's no identity, no ego. Life is an adventure which is constantly unfolding. You may find yourself laughing more.

Everything happens more smoothly when there's no John or Frida to get in the way. There's just a vast, empty space in which things happen.

Once you surrender, your inner image will bother you less and less

In the last chapter I talked about your *inner image* (or self-image) as opposed to your *outer image*, which you project to others, as though you're wearing a mask. (As you may remember, my inner image was 'I'm unacceptable', while my outer image was 'I'm clever and friendly'.)

The gap between the *inner image* and the *outer image* causes all kinds of problems. Fortunately, when we complete and surrender, our low inner image becomes *inactive*. It's there as a piece of historical information which we may think about from time to time, but it no longer causes us pain or runs our life.

For example, when I complete and surrender, I let go of my identity as John Purkiss and just flow. One thing happens after another, with no worries about what's going to happen to John Purkiss, what other people think about John Purkiss, etc. It's far more enjoyable than the old restricted way of living.

I encourage you to surrender and experience this for yourself.

Surrender will change the way you see yourself and the world

I often meet people who are stuck, through my work and in my social life. I can feel their pain and frustration, but I know they need to let go. Holding on is preventing things from happening in their lives.

Most of us have been conditioned to believe that we're a mind and a body, and that the only way to get things done is to think and work hard. Our modern culture encourages us to see ourselves as separate individuals. We're all working away trying to get what we want, in the hope that we'll be happy when we do – at some point in the future. Eventually we discover that it doesn't work. Fortunately, there's an alternative, which is to surrender.

You may be wondering what will happen if you surrender. A materialist might say that if you let go completely then your life will fall to pieces. However, my experience in Paris – and my friend's experience in the Mediterranean – suggest the opposite: when we let go completely, *things fall into place. Life unfolds naturally.*

Surrender isn't the same as giving up or doing nothing. It just means that we stop trying to make the world conform to our fixed ideas about how things should be. When we surrender we create space for something much more exciting to happen. This raises an obvious question: What's the 'something else' that makes everything happen?

The answer is beyond time and space. It's *beyond name and form.* So it's pointless trying to name or describe it, but that hasn't stopped people from trying. Here are 32 examples, in alphabetical order:

- **The Absolute**
- **Brahman (the ultimate reality underlying all phenomena)**
- **The cosmic energy**
- **The cosmic force of evolution**
- **The cosmic intelligence**
- **The cosmos**
- **The dance of creation**

- The Divine
- The divine consciousness
- Divine energy
- Existence
- The flow of life
- God
- A higher power
- Infinite intelligence
- Life
- The life force
- Nature
- The Self (with a capital S, as opposed to the individual self, with a small s)
- The Supreme
- The Supreme Being
- The Tao (or Dao)
- 'That'
- That which is beyond name and form
- Unity
- The universal consciousness
- The universal energy
- The universal flow
- The universal force
- The universal intelligence
- The universe
- The whole.

In this book I've used the term *Existence* to refer to *that which is beyond name and form*. It's easier to surrender once we realize that we're part of Existence and it's constantly supporting us.

When you surrender, the only thing you're giving up is your ego

The English verb *to surrender* is derived from the French verb *se rendre*, which means to give oneself up. The self in question is the self with a small s – in other words, the ego: our habit of identifying with the body and/or the mind. We're giving up our ego. If we keep surrendering, the ego becomes weaker and weaker. Life flows more and more smoothly.

The Western view of the ego has been heavily influenced by the work of Sigmund Freud (1856–1939). In his model of the psyche, the *id* contains instinctual drives – including sexual ones – while the *super-ego* is the moral conscience. The *ego* is the realist, trying to satisfy the *id*'s desires in ways that will bring pleasure rather than pain. The Eastern view is much older and totally different. It's shared by traditions such as Buddhism, Kabbalah, Sufism and the Vedas. In this book I'm applying the Eastern definition:

The ego is the illusion that you're separate from Existence

You feel cut off from everyone and everything, separate in your own body and mind. Maybe you feel superior in some way. Maybe you feel *inferior*. It's all ego.

One of the underlying messages of the Vedas – and of this book – is that you *aren't* the body or the mind. The body and the mind both come and go. They aren't *you*. You're *pure consciousness*, which *witnesses* the body changing and thoughts coming and going. You witness pain and thoughts, but you aren't your feelings or your thoughts. You can therefore let them come and go.

Ultimately, you have a choice. You can either:

1. **Try to achieve everything through mental and physical effort.**

2. **Surrender and follow your intuition, only thinking and taking action when necessary.**

For many people, option 1 works well for years or even decades. They're intelligent and good at what they do. They work hard and life turns out fine.

However, at some point option 1 stops working. We run into a wall, or what *seems* like a wall.

Many of us get frustrated, angry or depressed. We can't go any further. We feel stuck and life is terrible.

Eventually, some of us realize that it isn't a wall – it's a big step. If we want to keep moving forwards, we have to go up a level. And we realize we need to let go of something before we can do that.

Once we figure out what we need to let go of, we move up to another level and keep moving forwards for a while, until we hit another wall. That's how it's been for me, up a long flight of steps.

This process of moving up from one level to another is all about *letting go*, not acquiring.

We let go of judgements, labels, painful memories, mental patterns, preconceptions and so on. The higher we go, the further we can see. We feel lighter and things happen more easily.

REMEMBER TO SURRENDER

We may still lapse into the old way now and then and find ourselves trying to 'achieve' things through mental and physical effort, but it's painful, which wakes us up. Then we surrender again. Here's the cycle we go through:

Just to recap, the ego in the diagram opposite is the *false self*, which fools us into thinking we're separate, so we believe that the person in our stories is 'achieving' things through mental and physical effort. These are the stages in the cycle:

1. Surrender

You let go completely. You immerse yourself in what you're doing and allow things to unfold naturally. At some point you experience...

2. Joy

You feel relaxed. Life takes care of itself. Sooner or later, something wonderful happens. You feel excited, grateful and fulfilled. However, this quickly leads to...

3. Ego

You start believing that your body/mind was responsible for what happened. People congratulate you on your 'achievements'. You start to see yourself as separate from the whole, and go back to your old approach. This leads to...

4. Pain

Trying to do everything through mental and physical effort is tiring and stressful – and produces very patchy results. Life keeps pushing you to let go. At some point you experience a massive setback. Once you've suffered for a while you decide to...

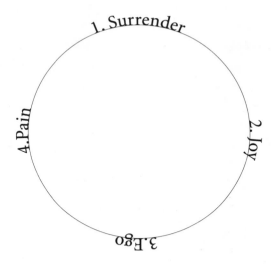

Initially, each cycle may take a few months or years to complete. My experience is that it gets shorter and shorter. After a while, you may go through the whole cycle in a day, a few hours or even a few minutes. Eventually, after repeated cycles, we surrender continuously.

You may be asking yourself, 'If I surrender, how will I know what to do?' The answer is that:

Once you surrender, your intuition will *tell* you what to do

Once you surrender, you can relax and enjoy the process. Your mind will become quieter because you're no longer resisting what's happening now, harking back to the past or fantasizing about the future. Then your intuition will tell you what to do.

Some people worry that, if they surrender, they'll become disorganized. Many of us pride ourselves on being well-organized – I like it too. It saves time, removes stress and makes life more enjoyable. However, there's no conflict between surrender and organizing things in your professional and personal life. If you surrender, your intuition will tell you when it is and isn't necessary. You'll organize things faster when your mind is clear.

Don't mistake incompletions for intuition

If you're present you can observe thoughts as they arise, as I described in chapter 2 (see page 33). However, the question is, are those thoughts coming from your intuition or from incompletions? Some people think they're using their intuition when they're really acting out of fear and incompletion. They're being triggered by unconscious pain patterns which haven't been completed. The way to avoid this is to make sure you keep completing the pain which is stored in your system – as I described in chapter 3, pages 105–19. Intuition is based on love, not fear.

When we surrender and fall into the present, we let go of worry

A friend of mine volunteers in the Scouts. Part of her role is to make sure the young people stay safe. She used to worry about what might happen and in her own words, 'overdid it and almost spoiled the fun'. These days she surrenders, falls into the present and remains aware of what's happening. Her intuition tells her when she needs to take action. She's now more effective in spotting and assessing real danger. In the meantime, she relaxes and enjoys her role.

Surrender allows things to happen in unexpected ways

When we surrender we stop trying to control *how* things happen. This enables them to happen more easily – often in unexpected ways. We can see this in every aspect of our lives. Here's an example:

My dad was a photographer and I've inherited his enthusiasm. I take photos using a digital camera or a mobile phone. For me there are two main approaches. The first is to think about the picture I want and then take control and set things up accordingly. The second approach is to walk around and see what happens. In other words, I surrender.

The best photos almost always come from the second approach. Sometimes things align for a second or two – maybe only a split second – and a perfect composition appears on the memory card. I may not even see the final image on the screen or through the viewfinder. It goes straight from three dimensions to the memory card. Surrender allows things to happen in unexpected ways.

Surrender during conversations

Some people try to control conversations. They label other people's comments as inappropriate, sexist, racist or whatever. Conversations like this usually achieve nothing.

It's better to let go and listen with an open mind. While you're listening you'll notice thoughts and feelings that come up in reaction to what other people are saying. There may be labels or judgements.

You may notice that your mind is rehearsing counter-arguments or preparing what you're going to say the moment they finish speaking. It's best to observe this mental chatter and let it go.

If you surrender during conversations, you may notice some remarkable changes:

- **You'll get on better with whoever you're listening to.**
- **Eventually, you may find yourself listening in what feels like an empty space. There are no separate people – only sounds and images which appear and disappear. Then there are thoughts and feelings which appear and disappear. You just notice whatever comes up and let it go.**
- **You learn a lot.**
- **New ideas appear during the conversation. They can come from either person – it doesn't matter who.**

It's best to *be empty* and *listen.* Allow the other person to talk. When they've finished speaking, it may or may not occur to you to say something. Sometimes the best response is silence. Sometimes it's best to ask a question, so you can understand what they're saying in more detail. All you have to do is let go and be present.

Try showing up with no agenda

If someone invites me to a meeting, I frequently go with no agenda. I do my homework on whoever I'm going to meet, and the organization where they work, but that's all. Then I listen very carefully to what they have to say, without interrupting or replying. I allow as much space as possible for new things to happen. Often, ideas appear for projects we can work on together.

This is how my friend Laurence Shorter describes his coaching work:

> When I'm coaching someone, I leave things open for chance. And I have found that when I'm most relaxed, most unattached to any outcome whatsoever, that's when things go best.
>
> All of this requires me to be more interested in feeling relaxed than in creating value for the client. And when I can show up that way, value always comes. It's the paradox of all good work.

'How can I let go/surrender in my job – when specific targets and deadlines have to be met?'

If you work for someone else and find yourself in this situation, you have two options:

1. Keep thinking about how you're going to meet the target/deadline. Take lots of action. Notice the results you're getting. Adjust your course of action. Take lots more action. And so on.
2. Acknowledge the target/deadline. Surrender. Do whatever your intuition tells you to do.

When I was in my 20s, I mainly followed the first approach, in accordance with my conditioning (upbringing, education, training). It was very stressful.

Since learning to surrender I've followed the second approach – including in a large company working directly for the chairman. It works *much* better. In some cases, the people who've imposed the target/deadline get stressed. I remain present, doing what needs to be done – quickly and efficiently (most of the time).

I invite you to try this for yourself.

If you're present and let go, there will be helpful coincidences

Many of us have noticed periods in our lives when everything seemed to flow naturally, without any major obstacles. If you're present and you let go, this may happen frequently. People appear at just the right time. Circumstances change. Things fall into place. It can feel uncanny and send a shiver down your spine.

You may have heard people say 'There are no coincidences' or 'There's no such thing as coincidence'. This is based on a linguistic misunderstanding.

Coincidence simply means that two things happen at the same time. It *doesn't* mean it's random or accidental. At the deepest level there's no separation: cause and effect are one. Things unfold, sometimes in ways that the mind struggles to comprehend or explain. But we don't need to worry about the mind. We can just let go.

Embrace uncertainty

Many of us are afraid of uncertainty – a lot of investors are. Whenever there's a crisis, people sell their investments in a hurry. Even when there isn't a crisis, many of us try to remove uncertainty from our lives in the hope of feeling 'safe' one day. The certainty we're pursuing is a mirage – life is uncertain.

As you practise the exercises in this book, you'll become more comfortable with uncertainty. In the beginning you may see yourself as a separate body/mind trying to make your way through life. The more you let go of the thoughts and feelings that have been holding you back, the more you'll realize that you *aren't* separate. Keep surrendering and everything will flow.

SUMMARY

- Now you've explored how to be present, how to let go of thoughts and let go of pain, it's time to let go completely. This is sometimes called *surrender*.

- Let go of all expectations, memories and thoughts about the present. Follow your intuition and do whatever feels right, moment by moment. Don't think about the outcome, just immerse yourself in whatever you're doing and enjoy it. See page 134 for more detail.

- When you surrender, you'll *fall into the present*. You'll tune in to what's happening now.

- When you surrender, you'll let go not only of your stories but of the person in the stories.

- You're pure consciousness – also known as pure awareness, pure presence or pure being.

- When you surrender you'll make space for new things to happen. We're all part of Existence, which is constantly supporting us.

- You may be in the habit of trying to achieve everything through mental and physical effort. Instead, you can surrender and follow your intuition, only thinking and taking action when necessary. Then you'll feel joy – you'll feel relaxed, excited, grateful and fulfilled. At some point you'll probably relapse into struggle and effort, but then you'll remember to surrender once more.

- Beware of false intuition. Make sure you keep completing your pain patterns using the exercises on pages 105–19.

- When you surrender in conversations – when you allow yourself to be empty and listen – you'll get on better with other people and learn a lot.

5

HOW TO TURN YOUR DESIRES INTO REALITY BY LETTING GO

So far I've talked about how to:

1. **Let go of thoughts**
2. **Let go of pain**
3. **Let go completely.**

Now it's time to come back to the question I asked you right at the beginning: 'What do you want to change in your life?'. In other words, which desires do you want to turn into reality?

For years I struggled to turn my desires into reality and I realized that many other people were in a similar situation. It was a big puzzle and I kept looking for the answer.

I investigated lots of concepts which you may also know about. There was 'The Secret', based on the 'law of attraction', taught by Esther and Jerry Hicks, which essentially said that you attract what you think about. Then there was Bärbel Mohr's book *The Cosmic Ordering Service*. The fundamental problem was that I couldn't get these concepts to work for me. They made sense in theory, but I was clearly missing something when I tried to put them into practice. Now it all makes sense, so I'll explain it as clearly as I can.

You may have heard the phrase 'The inner determines the outer'. The 'outer' is the material world, where we want things to happen. The 'inner' is your 'inner space'.

Whatever you hold in your *inner space* is what you create outside

Unless you're enlightened, your inner space is far from empty. It contains lots of pain patterns/incompletions – which I described in chapter 3. As long as they remain in your inner space, they'll keep manifesting in the world around you – in the form of things you don't want. As you may recall from that chapter:

We manifest our *beliefs*, not our *desires*. Once you're complete, your beliefs and desires become one. Then your desires start to become reality.

I'll start by talking about your desires. Then I'll explain what you can do to turn them into reality.

WHERE DO DESIRES COME FROM?

Many of us spend our lives trying to turn our desires into reality without addressing this fundamental question, so let's do so now. We can divide desires into three categories:

1. Desires that come from the ego

When we identify with the body/mind, we're in the grip of the ego and often pursue desires based on fear. This can include eating as much food as possible, out of an unconscious fear that there won't be enough in the near future. It can also include making as much money as possible because we're afraid of some other threat to our physical wellbeing. (There's nothing wrong with food or money, but our attitude to them is revealing.)

If we see ourselves as the body/mind we may also pursue what's known as 'name and fame'. We know that the body is going to die, so we try to build some fabulous reputation in the hope that

John Purkiss or Frida Smith will be remembered. Or we try to become famous in this lifetime, in the hope that it will bring us some other physical or mental benefit. Pursuing ego-based desires puts us on a hamster wheel. So long as we see ourselves as the body/mind, whatever we acquire will never be enough.

2. Borrowed desires

These are desires which we've 'borrowed' from other people. For example, it could be a desire to have a big car because other people want or have big cars, or a desire to have children because other people want or have children. If we look inwards and are honest with ourselves, we can see which desires we've borrowed from someone else. They're part of our social and cultural conditioning. Some people have been conditioned to want a house or lots and lots of money. Others have been conditioned to want a knife or a gun. Our 'shoulds' and expectations are based on this conditioning.

3. Desires that arise naturally

Once we remove ego-based desires and borrowed desires we're left with desires that arise naturally. They range from the desire to eat something within the next few hours to the desire to create something or experience something – whatever it may be. These desires simply occur in us.

WHY ARE SOME DESIRES REALIZED BUT NOT OTHERS?

If your inner space is pure consciousness, natural desires are realized easily. However, in most cases, our inner space contains lots of incompletions, which are to do with what we *don't* want. We've come to the wrong conclusions about ourselves, other people and the world around us. When this happens, we manifest our negative beliefs instead of manifesting our natural desires.

If you look carefully at your life, you can see what's happening. As I mentioned in the introduction, most of us are worried or feel stuck in one or more areas of our lives. So we keep struggling with the same issues, whether it's ill health, poor relationships, career frustrations or lack of money. Here are some examples:

- **You keep getting depressed.**
- **You frequently overeat and put on weight, increasing the risk of diabetes, heart disease and cancer.**
- **You move from one organization to another, running into the same problems with your colleagues each time.**
- **You've had the same problem or similar problems in one relationship after another.**
- **You're in what feels like a dead-end job and you don't know what to do about it.**
- **You want to build a team, raise money and start a business, but it never works out.**
- **You're good at what you do, but you keep running short of money.**
- **Whenever you have money, it always seems to leave you.**

None of these are random processes. These patterns of 'stuckness' repeat themselves in a way which is particular to each of us, because we each have our own particular incompletions. As I said in chapter 3, incompletions are incidents, memories and wrong cognitions from the past that are occupying the present and are affecting our future.

Writing down what you want to happen will show you what's *stopping* it from happening

One of the most popular, free courses run by Swamiji's *sangha* (community) is Kalpataru™ – named after a wish-fulfilling tree in Hindu scriptures. The course includes an exercise in which you write down *one thing* that you want to happen in your life, which hasn't happened yet.

If you do this, and then sit quietly and turn inwards, your mind will tell you all the reasons why it can't happen:

What's stopping your desires from happening?

Sit quietly on your own, with a pen and a sheet of paper, and no mobile phone or other distractions.

At the top of the page, write down something that you really want to happen in your life.

Now sit in silence and listen carefully. Your mind will start telling you why it can't happen. Please write it all down.

Here are some examples:

- I'm too old

- I'm too young

- I don't have enough money

- I'm not clever enough

- I'm not strong enough.

All these reasons why it can't happen are incompletions/pain patterns.

Now look at each incompletion you've written down – one at a time.

Do the completion exercise (see also page 105) with each of them:

Identify the incident when each pain pattern started. What happened? Write it down. Re-live each incident – at least five times – by talking to the person in the mirror. Feel it thoroughly, for as long as necessary.

If you want, you can then imagine the incompletions being burned away. You can even burn the papers on which you've written your incompletions. You can also imagine yourself dropping your incompletions at the feet of your guru.

Whatever you do, re-live the experience intensely from beginning to end.

Allow everything that makes you powerless to come to the surface and leave your system.

Feel it intensely and let it go. As I mentioned in chapter 3, the *decision* to complete is more than 80 per cent of the battle. Once we *decide* to complete, it begins to happen.

You're creating lots of space for new things to happen!

Once you've done this, the thing you want to happen will materialize more easily.

You also need to complete with your resistance

Many of us think or say we want something to happen, but deep down we're resisting it. If we really want it to happen, we have to complete with the resistance as well.

Let's go back to our four categories and imagine you want the following:

1. **Good health**
2. **A relationship**
3. **A well-paid job**
4. **Financial abundance.**

Let's imagine that none of them is happening, so you turn inwards and search for the resistance – the negative thought patterns about what it will take to turn these desires into reality, and what might happen as a result. Here are some examples:

Good health:

'I'll have to start exercising. I *hate* exercising.'

'I really don't like raw vegetables. I much prefer pizza and ice cream.'

'People will think I'm antisocial if I drink less alcohol, or give up altogether. They'll think I'm boring.'

A relationship:

'I don't have time for a girlfriend/boyfriend.'

'What if I tell them all my secrets and they betray me?'

'I feel unattractive.'

A well-paid job:

'I don't want to be tied to my desk.'

'I don't want to be responsible for lots of people.'

'I'd rather finish writing my book.'

Financial abundance:

'I'm not good with money.'

'Rich people are never happy.'

'Being rich will mess up my relationships. I won't be able to trust anyone.'

These pain patterns are all stopping what you want to happen from happening. Please deal with each of them in turn:

Go back in time and identify when this pain pattern started. (It could be a long time ago.) What's the incident in the past which is triggering these negative thoughts now?

Complete that experience by re-living it now.

Build completion into your daily routine

It's best to set aside time and do regular completion sessions. This is spiritual work. It's the equivalent of push-ups, swimming or walking up flights of stairs. If you do it regularly, your life will change.

I often complete last thing at night, before I go to bed. I sleep a lot better as a result. If you're still doing the gratitude exercise (see page 90), it's best to do the completion exercise beforehand.

First, you use completion to remove the pain patterns, and then you write down what you're grateful for. You'll go to bed feeling powerful!

This is how you'll be able to tell that completion is starting to work for you:

- It becomes harder to remember the thing(s) that used to cause you so much pain.
- You no longer feel powerless when you come into contact with other people.
- You feel lighter and/or happier, for no apparent reason.
- Things start changing and happening in your life.

You can actively seek out the source of your incompletions, so your desires are realized faster

Believe it or not, completion can be fun. It's a bit like clearing out your apartment to make space for nice, new furniture.

You get rid of painful memories and out-of-date thought patterns, so something new and exciting can happen. It could be:

- A specific incident that happened many years ago or two minutes ago. Either way, you *re-live* (not remember) the incident and feel any powerlessness from beginning to end.
- A bad feeling about yourself or someone else, or the situation in which you find yourself. It's remarkable how quickly life changes once we start systematically completing. Painful memories, thoughts and feelings no longer spoil the present moment or destroy the future.

Notice what happens when you complete

Re-live the experience from beginning to end. Feel any pain, irritation or discomfort that comes up.

Notice when things suddenly open up and start happening, when you weren't really thinking about it.

Make a note to remind yourself.

Good things start to happen when you seek out your incompletions. For example:

Completion affects the people around you

A friend of mine who'd learned completion began to experiment with it – in a friendly, relaxed way. She decided to look out for people and situations that would help her to resolve her incompletions.

After a highly competitive admissions procedure, she embarked on a graduate degree programme at a famous university. In her first week, while she was sitting in a crowded lecture theatre, she scanned the room to see if she felt uncomfortable about anyone. One particular person seemed to have been ignoring her all week.

She completed with the feeling of being ignored and excluded by him and his friends – without saying anything to any of them. The very next day he suddenly turned to her and said good morning. The following day he saved her nameplate – which she'd left behind – and brought it to her at another lecture. They've been on excellent terms ever since.

She repeated the completion process with all the other people with whom she felt an aversion or attraction. She felt calm and being in class was effortless. She also received many compliments from her classmates about her interactions with them during the course.

Completion changes the world around you

This same friend continued to experiment with completion. After moving into a waterfront apartment complex, she found that the exit gates were automated. It wasn't clear that they would continue to work in the case of a fire or flood. Only the building caretaker who worked in the mornings had a key to the manual lock on the emergency gate.

Month after month she lobbied to get a copy of the key as a safety precaution. Neither the property agents nor the building administrators provided one. Finally, she decided to apply completion to her feelings about the situation. She completed with everyone involved and with her fear of being imprisoned during an emergency.

The very next morning, after a ten-month campaign, the property agents called her out of the blue to announce that they had a key ready for her at no charge.

LET GO OF FIXED IDEAS ABOUT HOW YOUR DESIRE IS GOING TO BE REALIZED

Many of us know what we *want* to happen, but have fixed ideas about *how* it's going to happen. Here are some examples:

- You want a relationship, and assume it will be with *this particular* man or woman.
- You want more money, and assume it's going to come from a better job.
- You develop a product, which you assume will be used for a particular purpose.
- You want to start a business, and assume it will be in a particular sector.
- You want to share an idea, and assume it will be via a book rather than a video.

It's better to be clear about *what* you want to happen – and open-minded about *how* it will happen. Don't cling to anyone or anything. Allow other people to follow their own paths.

Follow your intuition and allow your desire to be realized in the way that works best for everyone.

Allow things to happen in unexpected ways

There are many examples of this in business: highly successful products and companies that started out as one thing and became another. Here are just three:

Post-it Notes

In 1968 Dr Spencer Silver, a chemist at 3M, was trying to develop a super-strong adhesive, but developed a very weak one instead. In 1974 a fellow 3M employee, Arthur Fry, had the idea of using the new adhesive to hold bookmarks in his hymn book while singing in the church choir. Post-it Notes are now sold in more than 100 countries.

The webcam

This was developed in 1991 in the Computer Science department at Cambridge University. The first webcam was set up by Dr Quentin Stafford-Fraser and Dr Paul Jardetzky to monitor a coffee pot in the corridor, so they didn't have to get up from their desks to see if there was coffee available. Webcams are now mass-produced and are a standard feature in laptop computers.

Instagram

In 2009 Kevin Systrom built a prototype app called Burbn which allowed users to check in online from a particular location, and post their plans and photos. After Mike Krieger joined him, they realized that users weren't using the check-in features at all, but they were posting and sharing enormous numbers of photos. Mike and Kevin decided to simplify the app while also giving users the ability to build a social network online. It quickly became one of the world's most successful social networking sites and was acquired by Facebook.

If you're developing a new product or service, it's best to keep an open mind. It may evolve into something you've never imagined.

The same principle applies in every area of our lives. You may already be clear about what you want to happen. It's best to keep an open mind about how it's going to happen – and with whom.

When we let go, we allow our desires to be realized in the best possible way

Before I discovered the processes I've explained in this book, I spent years doing the following. Maybe you've had a similar experience:

1. You set a goal
2. You formulate an action plan
3 You take lots of action
4 You try to get other people to do what you want them to do (which annoys some of them)
5. If the plan doesn't work, you formulate a new plan and start again.

It's demoralizing and exhausting. Years can go by and you're no further forward. These days my approach is completely different:

1. When you have an idea for something you'd love to happen, write it down at the top of a sheet of paper.
2. Close your eyes, turn inwards, and listen to your mind telling you all the reasons why it can't happen. Write it all down.
3. Go back and identify the painful experiences which you haven't completed – which are generating all the pain, discomfort, agitation and resistance.
4. Complete these experiences. *Re-live to relieve.*
5. Surrender and follow your intuition. It will tell you what to do.

SUMMARY

- We manifest our beliefs, not our desires. Once you're complete, your beliefs and desires become one. Then your desires start to become reality.

- Most of us have lots of incompletions in our inner space. That's why we feel stuck in one or more areas of our lives: health, relationships, career or money.

- If you have a desire that isn't happening, turn inwards. Your mind will tell you all the reasons why it can't happen. These reasons are incompletions.

- Go back and identify the original incident that causes you to feel bad. Sit in front of a mirror and re-live the experience. Feel any pain, discomfort or agitation in your body.

- Set aside a time to do regular completion sessions – for instance, last thing each night.

- You can seek out the source of your incompletions, so your desires are realized faster.

- Completion can change other people's behaviour, your relationships and the world around you.

- Let go of fixed ideas about *how* your desire is going to be realized.

- Let go and allow your desires to be realized in the best possible way.

CONCLUSION

I hope you've enjoyed reading this book as much as I've enjoyed writing it. I'd like to conclude by summarizing the journey we've just taken together. Then you can decide what to do next.

Most of us want to change something in our lives. Instead of working harder and harder to do this, you can change your life much more easily by letting go. Then you'll follow your intuition and take the right action at the right time. Increasingly, you'll find yourself in the right place at the right time too.

The starting point for letting go is to be present – to keep bringing our attention back to the present moment. Many of us learn to do this through meditation or yoga. Others experience it when they're on the top of a mountain or in the depths of a forest. The mind falls still – if only for a few seconds – and we feel connected to Existence. Every time our attention wanders, we bring it back to the here and now.

Once we've learned to be present, we can take the first step. We start observing our thoughts and letting go of them. There are stories, labels, judgements, expectations, comparisons, conclusions and so on. Most are useless. Some are potentially harmful. The important thing is not to identify with them. They aren't you. Remember the observer standing on the bridge above a river in full flood. There's no need to be swept away. Once we've started letting go of chaotic thoughts, we can be grateful for life as it unfolds, moment by moment.

The second step is to let go of the pain that runs our lives. This requires us to look deep inside ourselves. We've all had painful experiences – many of them during early childhood – which continue to mess up our lives, years or even decades later. Unfortunately, we've suppressed these negative emotions. We may think or say we're fine, but we aren't living the lives we want. The solution is to go back and find the incident at the source of this pain pattern. Something happened which led you to draw an incorrect conclusion about yourself, other people or the world. That pain pattern is still running your life. It makes you powerless. Now it's time to connect with yourself by looking in the mirror and re-living the painful experience. Re-live to relieve. Once you've completed each experience, the pain pattern will lose its grip on you and your life will change for the better. I encourage you to keep digging out those incompletions and letting go of them.

The third step is to let go completely – otherwise known as surrender. When we surrender we fall into the present. What a relief. We stop identifying with the body/mind known as John Purkiss, Frida Smith or whoever. We become one with Existence. Everything flows. We don't need to worry about the past or the future. We follow our intuition and everything falls into place – often in unexpected ways.

Once you've let go completely, your desires will become reality much more easily than before. Whatever you hold in your inner space is what you create outside. If action is required, it's quick and efficient. Things start happening, sometimes very fast indeed.

This is a journey towards consciousness. We become conscious of the thoughts and the pain patterns which are holding us back – and we let go of them. When we let go completely, we realize we're consciousness itself.

Wishing you bliss and fulfilment.

JP

WHAT'S NEXT?

My aim in writing this book is to make the most useful information available to everyone, so you can fulfil your potential. My own journey has led me to explore all the major spiritual traditions. I've shared with you what has worked for me and many others. (People sometimes ask me how long it took to write this book. My standard response is: 'Over five thousand years.' In other words, I didn't invent any of it. My role has been to test each principle thoroughly and then explain it as clearly as I can.)

In the West in particular, many people have abandoned religion for various reasons. There's an expanding group who describe ourselves as 'spiritual, not religious'. Some people have had negative experiences with religion which have led to major incompletions. I've met a lot of people who could fairly be described as 'militant atheists'. Once I get to know them, they usually tell me about some traumatic event which has turned them off the whole subject of religion.

My view is that we should let go of our incompletions and find out for ourselves whether a particular principle or technique works in practice – regardless of where it came from. Then we can move forwards quickly and lead much more fulfilling lives.

During ten years of church and Sunday school I absorbed two principles which I've mentioned in this book:

1. **Our brains and bodies are part of something infinitely intelligent.**
2. **If we can't solve a problem intellectually, we can pray for a solution.**

The word *pray* is derived from the French verb *prier*, which means *to ask*. As you may recall, when I was completely stuck, living in Paris, I let go and asked to be guided. My life then changed dramatically for the better.

My next stop after Christianity was Buddhism. I attended classes which made me realize how chaotic my mind was. One of the other participants described his attempts at mindfulness as 'chasing a butterfly with a bulldozer'. It wasn't until a few years later that I stumbled upon a simple technique that worked – which I've described on page 105.

I practised mindfulness for six years, and then learned Transcendental Meditation (see page 44) with the Maharishi Foundation. Pure consciousness made me see other human beings – and animals – in a new way. I felt a much stronger connection with them. I realized that the same consciousness is in all of us – regardless of any thoughts or emotions which keep appearing and disappearing within consciousness.

The next meditation technique I tried comes from Islam: silent Sufi meditation. It was my first experience of moving my attention from my head to my heart – sometimes described as the longest journey in the world. At times I had physical sensations around my heart. Both Sufism and Kabbalah (the mystical aspect of Judaism) offer techniques to remove the ego – the *false self* which fools us into thinking that we're separate from everyone and everything.

Five years ago I was introduced to Sri Nithyananda Paramashivam (Swamiji) whom I've mentioned several times in this book. I found that his completion technique was highly effective in removing the pain patterns from which the ego is constructed. The more I let go of them, the more I experienced pure consciousness and bliss.

Swamiji is regarded by his followers as an *avatar*. I don't mean the blue-skinned creature from the movie. In the Hindu tradition, an *avatar* refers to a being who comes back to help others.

From Swamiji I learned the completion technique described in chapter 3. He's reviving the entire Vedic tradition, which is the ultimate source of both mindfulness and Transcendental Meditation. He and his *sangha* (community) run a wide range of programmes, many of which are free of charge. They include the completion technique and how to turn your desires into reality.

These teachings are available to everyone. All we need to do is let go of any preconceptions which are holding us back. I encourage you to do so.

Mindfulness

Mindfulness has become extremely popular. There are thousands of books and courses, one of the most accessible being the Headspace app (www.headspace.com). Its co-founder is Andy Puddicombe, a former Buddhist monk whom I met a few times when he was based in London. Headspace has since raised lots of money and moved to Los Angeles, where it's expanding rapidly. You can try the app for free. Some people who practise mindfulness let go of all thoughts for a few minutes at least. However, others struggle and give up. If your mind keeps wandering, you may wish to move on to...

Transcendental Meditation (TM)

I learned TM with the Maharishi Foundation, which was founded by Maharishi Mahesh Yogi. The UK website (www.uk.tm.org) has links to websites in many other countries. The beauty of TM is that (a) it's effortless, and (b) when you transcend there's only consciousness. If you practise TM twice a day, it gradually permeates the whole of your life, with many benefits including better health, happier relationships and more creativity.

Whichever route you take initially, I recommend you drop everything that's holding you back and go for it. It will transform you and the world around you.

The Power of Letting Go Book Club

You're welcome to join the discussion on Facebook at www.facebook.com/groups/thepoweroflettinggo

RECOMMENDED
READING
AND VIEWING

On being present

The Power of Now: A Guide to Spiritual Enlightenment by Eckhart Tolle

At the age of 29 Eckhart had a profound experience that led him to write *The Power of Now*. This book draws on several traditions.

Practising the Power of Now by Eckhart Tolle

This is a collection of extracts from *The Power of Now*. If you're new to Eckhart Tolle's work, you may wish to start with this book.

The Inner Game of Tennis by W Timothy Gallwey

Timothy Gallwey learned to meditate and found that his tennis improved. The 'inner game' is played against opponents such as nervousness and self-doubt. Peak performance occurs when the mind is still and at one with what the body's doing. His later books include *Inner Skiing* and *The Inner Game of Golf*.

On letting go of your story

Loving What Is: Four Questions That Can Change Your Life by Byron Katie, with Stephen Mitchell

Byron Katie 'discovered that when I believed my thoughts, I suffered, but that when I didn't believe them, I didn't suffer, and that this is true for every human being'. She explains how to do 'The Work', which relieves this suffering.

Who Would You Be Without Your Story?: Dialogues with Byron Katie

This book is a series of 15 dialogues with audience members who are doing 'The Work'. Having seen Byron Katie live, I can confirm how effective her teaching method is. You can download what you need to get started at www.thework.com.

On completion

If you type 'Nithyananda' and 'completion' into the search box on YouTube, you'll find many videos on this subject.

On the shadow/dark side

The Dark Side of the Light Chasers by Debbie Ford

We try to be good. In other words, we 'chase the light'. In the process we repress many aspects of ourselves, which become part of our dark side, otherwise known as the shadow. Debbie shows how to reintegrate your shadow and become whole.

On letting go of the urge to control

Tao Te Ching by Lao Tzu, translated by Stephen Mitchell.

This is an excellent translation of the *Tao Te Ching*, which dates back to the sixth century BCE and is normally attributed to Lao Tzu ('old master'), a record-keeper at the Zhou Dynasty court. An enjoyable read.

The Lazy Guru's Guide to Life by Laurence Shorter

The author and illustrator have distilled some of the great wisdom traditions into a few pages of entertaining text and cartoons. There's a simple, powerful exercise in three steps.

On oneness and the illusion of separation

Good Company by His Holiness Shantanand Saraswati

Shantanand Saraswati taught the philosophy of Advaita, usually translated as 'non-duality', 'not two' or 'one without a second'. *Good Company* is an anthology of 40 of his talks recorded between 1961 and 1985.

The Upanishads: A New Translation by Vernon Katz and
Thomas Egenes

An accessible translation of a very important text. *The Upanishads*
are also known as the Vedanta, meaning the end of the Veda, or
knowledge. The 20-page introduction explains the context and
principal themes.

Beyond Knowledge by Jean Klein, edited by Emma Edwards

Jean Klein was a philosopher of Advaita Vedanta, who taught
students to open themselves to their 'true nature: the "I am" of pure
consciousness'. He emphasized the direct way to knowledge,
without elaborate programmes or practices.

On mindfulness, kindfulness and Zen

Mindfulness for Dummies by Shamash Alidina

Shamash is a well-known mindfulness teacher. This is the first of
his books on the subject.

Kindfulness by Ajahn Brahm

This is an excellent, short book for anyone who wants to start
learning mindfulness on their own, or who's learned mindfulness
and got stuck. Ajahn Brahm shows how to overcome obstacles to
blissful meditation. Letting go is one of the underlying themes.

*Zen Mind, Beginner's Mind: Informal Talks on Zen Meditation and
Practice* by Shunryu Suzuki

Suzuki was a respected Zen master in Japan when he moved to the
United States in 1958. He became one of the most influential Zen
teachers of his time. This book will appeal to practitioners of any
form of meditation – not just Zen.

On Transcendental Meditation

Catching the Big Fish: Meditation, Consciousness, and Creativity by David Lynch

David Lynch is a film-maker whose work includes *The Elephant Man*, *Mulholland Drive* and *Blue Velvet*. This book describes how transcendence enables us to experience pure consciousness and creativity. Beautifully written.

Transcendence: Healing and Transformation Through Transcendental Meditation by Norman E Rosenthal

Norman Rosenthal is a clinical professor of psychiatry, and *Transcendence* is one of the best-known books on TM. It combines scientific evidence, case studies and interviews with Paul McCartney, Russell Brand, David Lynch and others.

Super Mind: How to Boost Performance and Live a Richer and Happier Life through Transcendental Meditation by Norman E Rosenthal

This book explains – both anecdotally and scientifically – how transcendence steadily permeates the daily lives of those who practise TM regularly. There are interviews with top performers such as Hugh Jackman (the Hollywood actor) and Ray Dalio (founder of Bridgewater Associates, the world's largest hedge fund).

Strength in Stillness: The Power of Transcendental Meditation by Bob Roth

Bob trained as a teacher of TM with Maharishi Mahesh Yogi in 1972 and has since become one of the world's most experienced meditation teachers. He is also the CEO of the David Lynch Foundation, which teaches at-risk adults and young people to meditate.

On enlightenment

Living Enlightenment by Paramahamsa Nithyananda

HDH Sri Nithyananda Paramashivam is an enlightened master who says in the introduction, 'Understand, Existence is trying to express itself through you. When you freely allow this, you will start realizing your infinite potential.' This book covers a wide range of topics in detail, with clear explanations of Sanskrit terms. You can download it for free from www.nithyananda.org.

On career management

How to Be Headhunted: The Insider's Guide to Making Executive Search Work for You by John Purkiss and Barbara Edlmair

Headhunting – or executive search – has long been shrouded in mystique. This book helps readers to market themselves to executive search consultants and be included on shortlists for the senior jobs that interest them.

Brand You by John Purkiss and David Royston-Lee

This book shows how to build a personal brand based on your talents, values and purpose. It then uses archetypes to help readers create a powerful brand identity which they can communicate both on and offline.

On surrender

The Surrender Experiment: My Journey into Life's Perfection by Michael A Singer

Mickey Singer was a doctoral student in economics when he learned to meditate. This led to a profound spiritual experience. He decided to surrender to life – and let go of self-centred thoughts and emotions. The results were extraordinary.

Drop Everything and Surrender by Paramahamsa Nithyananda

You can download this book as a PDF free of charge from www. nithyananda.org, either via this link (books.nithyananda.org/ product/drop-everything-surrender/) or by entering the title into the search box. On page 82 he writes, 'Surrender itself is enlightenment. At that moment you experience the Truth.'

Sri Nithyananda Paramashivam

His Divine Holiness Bhagawan Sri Nithyananda Paramashivam – known to his followers as Swamiji – is reviving the entire Vedic tradition from its original sources and making it accessible to everyone. The original source of the completion technique on page 105 is the ShivaJnana Upanishad, Vijnana Bhairava Tantra, 94th verse, 22nd technique.

You can download his new app from https://nlighten.tv. Further information is available from www.nithyanandauniversity.org.

AKNOWLEDGEMENTS

I would like to thank the following:

Jacq Burns, my writing coach and agent, for her continuous advice and feedback, through many drafts.

Kate Adams and Ella Parsons at Octopus for editing this book and making it happen.

Neil Lukover for teaching me Transcendental Meditation.

Shamash Alidina and Dr Norman Rosenthal for advising me on mindfulness and Transcendental Meditation respectively.

Nell Axelrod and Ping Xu for advising me on the Chinese proverb in chapter 2.

Mali Mizrahi and Marcus Weston for teaching me at the Kabbalah Centre.

Ivana Sretenovic for introducing me to HDH Bhagavan Sri Nithyananda Paramashivam.

Mahant Ma Nithya Atmadayanda for helping me to understand and apply his teachings.

Irene Brankin, David Royston-Lee and Adina Tarry for their advice on psychology.

Dr Susanna Sällström Matthews for her advice on economics and the scientific method.

Jeremy Marshall for his critique of the text from a Christian point of view.

Rose Alexander for her advice on intellectual property law.

The School of Philosophy and Economic Science (www.schoolofphilosophy.org), the Maharishi Foundation (www.uk.tm.org) and Nithyananda Dhyanapeetam (www.nithyananda.org) for their cooperation and permission to quote from their publications.

I'm also very grateful to everyone who has read various drafts and given me their feedback, or had ideas which have helped to make this book better. I apologize to anyone I've omitted – please contact me and I will include you in the next edition.

In the meantime, I would like to thank Gavin Andrews, Dr Afzana Anwer, Robert Ashdown, Nell Axelrod, Colin Beckley, Sofia Beloka, Adam Bennett, André Berry, Patricia Bidi, Emma Bondor, Paul Bramley, Olivia Cartier, Pierce Casey, Marion Chalmers, Charles Cooper, Sara Cooper, David Coulson, Julie Cross, Kully Dhadda, Dr Myrrh Domingo, Thomas Drewry, David Dwek, Dr Barbara Edlmair, Dr Mahnaz Emami, Salar Farzad, KT Forster, Dr Jonathan Freeman, Helen Gale, Liz-Ann Gayle, Mahdieh Ghasemi, Vishal Handa, Sara Haq, Laxmi Hariharan, Dr Barry Harrison, Melinda Alexander Haseth, David Head, Abigail Hunt, Hanadi Jabado, Joysy John, Matthew Johnson, Lydia Kan, Grace Kelly, Bali Kochar, Soonu Kochar, Rupert Konstam, Vinay Kulkarni, Francesca Lahiguera, Dr Ali Lehovsky, Teresa Loy, Vari McLuskie, Charles McDermott, Bruce McFee, Karen Macmillan, Anna Marietta, Dr Naazi Marouf-Key, Andrew Marstrand, Nitish Mital, Dr Lee Mollins, Glenn Moore, Andrea Moretti-Adimari, Caroline Morgan, Julie Nazerali, Dr Laura Nelson, Mohand Nekrouf, Safaa Nhairy, Darius Norell, Oz O'Neill, Jessica Ordovas Ussia, Helen Osborne, Caroline Palmy, Stephen Parry, Deepika Patel, Judy Piatkus, Margaret Purkiss, Simon Purkiss, Stéphane Rambosson, Nadia Rauf, Leya Reddy, Julian Robus, Anita Rolls, Wendy Rosenthal, David Royston-Lee, Joe Salem, Jenny Santi, James Scott, Dan Scoular, Sunita Sehmi, Nagila Selmi, Anita Shah, Sanjay Shah, Jana Sharaf, Jo Sharp, Sanam Singh, Jonathan Smith, Dr John Spackman, Ivana Sretenovic, Andrei Stepanov, Mirela Sula, Vandna Synghal, Clifford Thurlow, Kahéna Tlili-Fitzgerald, Andy Trott, Elisabeth Tschyrkow, Nikhil Vadgama, Rahima Valji, Krish Vells, Dr Preema Vig, Andrea von Finckenstein, Hema Vyas, Becky Walsh, Ashley Ward, Retno Widuri, John Williams, Nick Williams, Roger Wilson, Adele Winkley, Gillian Wood, Susanne Worsfold and Ping Xu.

NOTES

....

....

....

....

....

....

....

....

....

....

....

....

....

....

....

....

....

....

....

....

....
....
....
....
....
....
....
....
....
....
....
....
....
....
....
....
....
....

ABOUT THE AUTHOR

John Purkiss studied economics at Cambridge University and has
an MBA (Master of Business Administration) from INSEAD, where
he was awarded the Henry Ford II Prize. He began his career in
banking and management consultancy in London and Chicago,
and worked in sales and marketing in the UK and Continental
Europe. John then learned to meditate, which made his intuition
much stronger and enabled him to move into executive search, or
'headhunting'. He recruits chief executives, finance directors and
other board members. John is the co-author of *How to be
Headhunted* and *Brand You* (published by Pearson). He is a regular
speaker on executive search, personal branding and letting go.
www.johnpurkiss.com